THE
WIGAN
WARRIORS
MISCELLANY

EWAN PHILLIPS

The
History
Press

Dedication

To the Wigan fans: jackpot winners in the lottery of
Rugby League life.

First published 2010

The History Press
The Mill, Brimscombe Port
Stroud, Gloucestershire, GL5 2QG
www.thehistorypress.co.uk

© Ewan Phillips, 2010

British Library Cataloguing in Publication Data.
A catalogue record for this book is available from the British Library.

ISBN 978 0 7524 5675 1

Typesetting and origination by The History Press
Printed in Great Britain
Manufacturing managed by Jellyfish Print Solutions Ltd

ACKNOWLEDGEMENTS

Huge thanks to the following: Kris Radlinski for his great foreword and swift responses to my irritating questions, Julie Baker and the team at the excellent new Museum of Wigan Life and Sue 'Mrs Francis' Francis for their archive materials, Michelle Tilling at The History Press for her encouragement and editing, Ray Hewson, Bill Francis, Ray Unsworth and Graham Emmerson for prompt responses to my queries, Jane and Tom for the tea and patience and, of course, Wigan RLFC itself for providing such a wealth of material and so many wonderful memories.

FOREWORD

By Kris Radlinski MBE

Wherever I travel in the world and people ask where I am from, my answer 'Wigan' always gets the same response: 'Oh Rugby League. I love that game.' The club's history transcends sports and countries; everybody has heard of the famous 'Cherry and Whites'.

In our little cobbled town Rugby League is a way of life; it's the main topic of conversation in pubs and the first choice of sport in the playgrounds. A recent survey showed that the two most common phrases used in a Wiganer's lifetime are 'gerrum onside' and 'can't run bout legs'. This is the language in which we speak. In the posh areas just outside Manchester, I've heard it said that within five minutes of meeting an attractive woman in a bar, she'll ask what car you're driving in order to assess your wealth. Not in Wigan, here she'd want to know what position you play and how many tackles you missed in your last game. These two statistics are far more important to the success of any budding relationship.

Everybody knows the Wigan players around town but they aren't treated any differently, there are no superstars and I wouldn't like it any other way. The fact that an old woman in a shopping centre can always vent her frustrations over a recent performance means your feet remain firmly planted on the ground. Players are accessible in Wigan; we don't opt to live out of town and travel in to train every day. To understand and appreciate the importance of Rugby League here you have to be in the middle of it and embrace the opinions of those who pay your wages each week. Yes, it can be a pain in the backside being nice to people who want to abuse you about how you played, but we must accept this as the Wigan supporters are special. Over the years, our success rate has slowed down but our fan base has gone up, underlining the fact that this is firmly a Rugby League town.

As a kid growing up I dreamed of playing at Central Park. Every weekend, with my family, I would sit on the old dugout two hours before kick-off waiting for my heroes to arrive. When the players did appear, I was in awe at the size and strength of these superhuman athletes and from an early age my mind was set on becoming one of them. To have actually realised my dreams and played there on so many occasions makes me feel incredibly lucky.

As I sit here writing this, I am looking out of the window at the current squad training, all with the same hopes and dreams as I had, I am so jealous and would love nothing more than to do it all again. Playing for this club doesn't just last from the day you sign until the day you leave; the truth is you never leave it. I have known players from Australia who were devastated to leave at the end of their contracts, they preferred the grey skies and warm pints of Wigan to their bikini-filled, sun-drenched beaches: crazy, but very true.

I have been associated with this club for nearly sixteen years and I have done every job imaginable. It only seems two minutes ago that I was in Central Park cleaning the first-team players' boots and, if I close my eyes and concentrate, I can still smell those old changing rooms. Now, in my current role, I am involved in making decisions that have a huge impact on players' careers, so I think about what people thought about me as a kid and what persuaded them to take a chance. I'll be looking for kids with a burning ambition to succeed, who understand the club and who will represent the jersey in the tradition it deserves. The club has been great with me and I will serve it the best way I can until my famous bright red hair has turned silver. Enjoy the book.

Kris Radlinski, 2010

THE ORIGIN OF THE 'SPECCIES'

Wigan's first rugby club, the imaginatively titled Wigan FC, was formed on 21 November 1872 at the Royal Hotel, Standishgate (now a branch of WH Smith). Nine days later, the fifty or so founding members played each other in the opening 'fixture' on the charmingly named Folly Field, Upper Dicconson Street. The venture's first proper competitive match was a trip to Warrington on 18 January 1873, which ended in a draw (no doubt there was a fight).

In 1876, financial problems and the difficulty of attracting new players led to a merger with Upholland FC, creating the all-new Wigan and District Football Club. The new club's games were played at the then Wigan Cricket Club ground in Prescott Street but it folded again within eighteen months.

22 September 1879 saw another relaunch and with it, a bold rebranding: the club was now to be called Wigan Wasps. Go-getting player-secretary Jack Underwood negotiated a return to Folly Field for an annual rental fee of £2.50 and the 'Wasps', in blue and white hooped jerseys promptly lost their opening home game to Chorley St Lawrence by the margin of six tries and two touchdowns to Wigan's one try, one touchdown and one dead ball (whatever all that means). However, the Wasps – the present club's direct ancestor – soon developed a 'buzz' about them and thrived well enough to move back to a ground of their own, Prescott Street, in 1886. In September of that year they took on and beat Wakefield Trinity in front of 5,000 paying 'speccies' and in 1888, they were given the accolade of a match with a touring New Zealand Maori side who won 8–1 in front of a 7,000 crowd.

By 1894, Wigan's ambition led to incursions beyond the environs of Platt Bridge and Goose Green in search of playing talent and brought accusations from Salford that they had paid one of their players – Miles – 30s a week during the summer. Wigan denied the allegations but were found guilty, Miles was labelled a professional and the club earned a three-month suspension. This led to their joining with similarly wronged teams at the George Hotel, Huddersfield, in September 1895 to form the breakaway Northern Union. Soon after, Wigan played their first fixture in the new code away to Broughton Rangers, winning 9–0.

Both Wigan and the new game proved instant crowd-pullers and in 1901, they moved grounds again to Springfield Park – later home to Wigan Athletic of course – where they became League Champions, winning 21 out of 24 fixtures. However, the owners of the ground wanted too large an increase in rent the following year, so in 1902 the club purchased a long-term lease on a plot of land just off Powell Street that was being used for grazing by Joe Hill, a local butcher. The handily located site was owned by the Great Central Railway Company and – in a naming rights forerunner – they stipulated the company name should be reflected in the new ground's title, so the name Central Park and something of a dynasty was born.

MOST TRIES FOR WIGAN

1	478	Billy Boston
2	368	Johnny Ring
3	312	Brian Nordgren
4	274	Shaun Edwards
5	258	Jimmy Leytham
6	241	Ernie Ashcroft

7	231	Eric Ashton
8	223	Jack Morley
9	189	Ellery Hanley
10	187	Johnny Lawrenson
11	186	Martin Offiah
12	185	Gordon Ratcliffe
13	183	Kris Radlinski

THE WHITE 'VAN' MEN

In the 1920s, the Wigan directors became so fond of signing accomplished South African Rugby Union players that opposing fans began disparagingly referring to the club's home ground as 'Springbok Park'. Barely a week seemed to pass without the local press trumpeting another exotic purchase's arrival in drooling terms that usually ended in the phrase 'looks like a fine specimen of manhood'. The reason for the fad was the incredible success of the club's first two Cape crusaders: flying winger Adriaan Jacobus 'Attie' van Heerden, a motorbike-riding heart-throb who brought the club its first taste of real star quality, and uncompromising second row Gert Wilhelm 'George' van Rooyen, a man seemingly responsible for more incredible feats of strength than a character from Greek myth.

Van Heerden quickly made an impression at Wigan using his Olympic hurdling skills to score spectacular long-range tries and develop a reckless habit of leaping over opponents. His famous try in the 1924 Challenge Cup final has gone down in Rugby League history, but just four days after that he touched down four times against Hunlset with one of his efforts involving the beating of eight men for what is still regarded as one of the greatest scores at Central Park. Ideally built – even by today's standards – at 6ft 1in and 13st 4lbs, his arrival in Wigan caused something of a stir. Contemporary reports describe townsfolk frequently just stopping to stare in admiration at the striking, hatless 'bonny lad' as he strode through Wigan. Such was his instant impact and iconic status in the town, his older brother Nicholas was temporarily persuaded to turn his back on a job as a doctor of dental surgery at the University of Michigan and try his luck at Central Park. It quickly became obvious that 'Van the Second', though also a decorated former hurdler back home, was not quite in Attie's league.

If 'AJ' was the rapier, Van Rooyen who stood at 6ft 2in and weighed in at just under 17st, was the bludgeon. A massive presence, known as 'Tank' or 'Tiny' and described as someone who 'tore down the pitch with the force of an avalanche', he was bought from Hull KR to 'strengthen the acknowledged weakness in the forward line' and clearly did that just by actually standing in it. It is said he could carry a bag of cement under each arm, nonchalantly clear snowy Central Park pitches with a 12ft x 7in wooden plank and once heaved a Corporation horse out of a manhole. He was also reported to have lifted a broken down van off its wheels to the point of almost turning it over, shouldered clear a Central Park crush barrier sunk more than 3ft into the ground and – in his Widnes days – swum across the River Mersey after missing the car transporter.

These two contrasting cult heroes played enormous roles in spreading Wigan's fame and broadening the club's scouting horizons, as well as, let's not forget, bringing in two Lancashire League Championship victories, a Challenge Cup win and an RL Championship.

TEN GREAT:
SUPER LEAGUE TRIES

25 August 1997, Jason Robinson
(Bradford 18 Wigan 33 at Odsal)

You may not be aware but England Rugby Union national treasure Jason Robinson actually used to play a bit of Rugby League for Wigan and this was one of his very best scores in the Cherry and White: collecting a kick 80m out, he ducked through one tackle, beat another, accelerated past a third defender on the outside and turned Stuart Spruce inside and out before storming in at the corner to continue Wigan's second-half fightback from 18–0 down. Sensational running or maybe the Bulls defence was just transfixed by those mercifully short-lived Wigan jerseys with the bizarre, swirly 'warrior' picture on the front.

24 October 1998, Jason Robinson
(Leeds 4 Wigan 10 at Old Trafford)

The inaugural Grand Final promised thrills, skills and Australian-style razzmatazz; it provided defence, handling errors and Manchester-style driving rain. The occasion needed something special and, as so often, Robinson provided it. Scampering away from acting half, he sped across field before knifing between Darren Fleary and Jamie Mathiou to scuttle past Iestyn Harris and score the only try of the game, and in doing so, secured himself the Harry Sunderland Award.

19 March 1999, Mick Cassidy
(Leeds 12 Wigan 26 at Headingley)

An unexpected name to see in any list of spectacular tries, but this does a disservice to Cassidy's ceaseless appetite for work.

Minutes after Paul Johnson had run 80m to kill off Leeds' spirit, Wigan produced a further, even more dazzling move to seal the win: Jason Robinson raced down the right touchline, passed to Radlinski before supporting on his inside to take the return pass and head out left where Cassidy was on hand to storm over in the corner and top an exhilarating support play master class.

27 August 2000, Kris Radlinski
(Wigan 20 Bradford 19 at the JJB Stadium)

This incredible last-second score was the first real moment of abandonment at Wigan's new stadium. Grown men forgot the horror of where they were and leapt speechlessly into the arms of total strangers in the manner of those joyous Central Park occasions down the years. In a game they needed to win to secure top spot, Wigan trailed all evening to a big, organised Bulls outfit, but as the clock ticked down, a pressurised Bradford lost two men to the bin and Wigan went for broke. There were 12 seconds left when Farrell's wide pass sent Renouf haring and dummying his way up the left wing, the scrum-capped centre perfectly timing his pass to Radlinski who had no guts left to bust in his marathon support run. With the game actually officially over, Farrell still had a thoroughly difficult angled conversion to win the game and it is a tribute to him that no one in the stadium ever really considered he wouldn't do it. It went over with his customary world-class lack of fuss and Wigan fans perhaps began to approach at least the 'end of the beginning' of their despair over the whole Tesco, football stadium and 'Warriors' stuff.

29 September 2000, Steve Renouf
(Wigan 16 St Helens 54 at the JJB Stadium)

What followed was too painful to recall, but Wigan actually had the perfect start with this gem of a try. Andy Farrell sliced straight through from 75m, handed on to Terry Newton on half way, the hooker continued the move and found Steve Renouf who straightened up before throwing in a beautiful step that took out two defenders and left him free to touchdown under the posts.

10 October 2003, Brian Carney
(Leeds 22 Wigan 23 at Headingley)

In terms of quality of rugby, this play-off semi-final is arguably the finest game in Wigan's still-short Super League existence and saw Irishman Brian Carney briefly looking like the best winger in the world. His first try, after just 6 minutes, saw him riskily allow a Leeds bomb to bounce close to his own 10m line, pluck the ball away from the very cuticles of the hotly pursuing Keith Senior, beat two men down the left wing and link up with Radlinski, who passed another two defenders before Carney accepted his return on the inside to score.

10 October 2003 (same game!), Brian Carney
(Leeds 22 Wigan 23 at Headingley)

This was clearly a night when Carney could do no wrong. His second score came on the hour mark after Radlinski had valiantly fought the ball back into play from in goal. The wing took the ball from acting half-back, spun out of a double tackle, accelerated away from Burrow and McDonald and tore the remaining 90m to the posts with Mathers and Cummins chasing in vain. One of the greatest Wigan tries of any era.

3 September 2004, Brian Carney
(Wigan 12 Leeds 12 at the JJB Stadium)

Carney's spectacular 2003 tries were still being talked of and broadcast in the build-up to this game almost a year later, so the genial wing clearly decided to provide a sequel and barely 2 minutes had elapsed when he burned off Senior and Mathers in a 75m touchline-hugging dash before diving over in the corner to add to the growing belief that Carney felt if it wasn't going to be brilliant, then it wasn't really worth scoring.

12 September 2004, Andy Farrell
(London 22 Wigan 26 at Griffin Park)

This try may not sound quite as spectacular as the other nine, but it was an effort that encapsulated the fighting qualities of Andy Farrell in the season where he won both Man of Steel and the Golden Boot. With his side looking lethargic at 18–22 down in a game they sorely needed to win to ensure a home play-off, the Wigan skipper, filling in at prop and clearly frustrated by the struggle around him, simply seized the game by the scruff of the neck. He dummied, brushed off two defenders and roared under the posts to lift his side and provide a lead they never lost.

11 August 2006, Mark Calderwood
(Leeds 18 Wigan 20 at Headingley)

An improbable winner from an underperforming winger against the club that let him go and quite simply, the try that meant Wigan weren't getting relegated. As Leeds were attacking the Wigan line, Calderwood seized on a stray pass and went 50m before being halted by the Leeds cover. From the play the ball, Chris Ashton (I wonder what became of him?) broke down the right wing, passed back to Calderwood and two lovely sidesteps later, he was over for a try that felt like it had won Wigan the league. It was a long final 15 minutes after that, mind.

CENTRAL PARK: DID YOU KNOW?

During the Second World War, Central Park was used as a training centre for the Home Guard, Air Training Corps and the Territorial Army. The pitch was used as a drill ground, a soldiers' billet was located under the Douglas Stand and one of the dressing rooms was used as a temporary gaol. Anti-aircraft guns were stationed on the Kop.

Central Park has hosted wrestling bouts, a concert by the Halle Orchestra, a horse riding display by a group of touring Cossacks and a baseball match between two teams of US soldiers stationed nearby. They called themselves the California Eagles and the New York Yanks (New York won 19 to 7 apparently).

The Good Friday derby on 27 March 1959 has gone down in history as Wigan's record attendance. 47,747 turned up at Central Park to see Wigan win 19–14. The gate receipts were £4,804.

Central Park was regarded as one of the major venues of Rugby League and hosted 21 Test matches, 2 World Club Challenges, 3 Challenge Cup finals (plus the home leg of the 1944 final), 4 Championship Finals, 5 Regal Trophy finals, 24 Lancashire Cup finals, 3 BBC2 Floodlit Cup finals, a Premiership Final and 22 Challenge Cup semi-finals.

In the 1962/63 season, Wigan went eleven weeks without a game due to a two-month 'Big Freeze' between December and March. Pneumatic drills had to be used to break up the 2in-thick layer of ice on the rink-like Central Park pitch and the players were forced to train on Blackpool Sands. The scene was something of a shock for the club's new Fijian signing, Kia Bose, who had just flown in from temperatures of 27°C and had never seen ice before.

When Central Park first opened, there were no dressing rooms, so players got changed in a nearby pub, the Prince of Wales in Greenough Street, and walked to the ground.

On 12 January 1952, a home game between Wigan and Wakefield became the first televised League match as the BBC stationed two cameras on the Douglas Stand to beam live pictures of the first half. Wigan led 16–3 after those 40 minutes with Ernie Ashcroft scoring a truly memorable 50m spectacular that history has now forgotten actually began with a slightly forward-looking pass.

Wigan inaugurated their impressive new £17,500 floodlights with a special game against Bradford Northern on 7 September 1967. Wigan fan and chart-topping singer Georgie Fame performed the kick-off, but the lights failed twice necessitating running repairs and meaning the game took 98 minutes to complete and ended 7–7.

100% CLUB

They may only have pulled on the Cherry and White once but they scored:

James Taylor (stand-off) 1 try v Oldham at Belle Vue	1st place play-off	19 April 1911
J.H. Halsall (centre) 1 try v Hull (a)	League	27 September 1941 (Liverpool Stanley player making wartime guest appearance)
James Robinson (centre) 1 try v Barrow (h)	League	14 April 1945 (Castleford player making wartime guest appearance)
Brian Ludbrook (centre) 1 try v Bramley (h)	League	27 September 1952
Tommy Vose (full-back) 1 try v Salford (a)	League	3 April 1961
Alan Jones (wing) 2 tries v Blackpool (h)	League	23 August 1961
Tony Byrne (hooker) 1 try v Batley (h)	League	27 September 1969
Darren Williams (wing) 1 try v Whitehaven (a)	2nd round Regal Trophy	14 November 1993

The feat has also been achieved by anonymous trialists on four occasions: 1924, 1942 (2 tries), 1943 and 1972. Wing James

Case kicked a goal on his only appearance v Huddersfield (h) on 7 October 1944 and David Highton landed seven goals from full-back against Liverpool City at Central Park in his one outing on 9 November 1957.

PLAYER OF THE DECADE: 1900–10

James Leytham (1903–12)

In the era of moustaches, baggy shorts and large boots, Jimmy Leytham became Wigan's first Rugby League superstar. A super-fast wing three-quarter whose trademark was kicking the ball past his opponent before racing round to re-gather and score, he signed from his home town of Lancaster in December 1903 for £80 (though Wigan later claimed to have secured him for the bargain fee of just £10). Jimmy went on to become Wigan captain and a genuine all-time great. Famed for his sporting behaviour, he was known to all as 'Gentleman Jim' and was such a skilful runner that he frequently walked off even the muddiest fields in immaculate kit as the opposition had been unable to successfully lay a hand on him.

Leytham marked his debut against Batley at Central Park on 12 December 1903 with a well taken try and, being a handy goalkicker too, had registered his 1,000th point by the time Wigan took on St Helens at Knowsley Road on 27 December 1909. Jimmy was very much 'The Hammer of the Saints' – his total of 28 tries in derby matches is a record that still stands today. He topped the Rugby League try charts three times between 1906 and 1910.

In November 1907 between 25,000 and 30,000 people crammed into Central Park to see Wigan take on the New

THE WIGAN WARRIORS MISCELLANY

Zealand tourists, captained by the brilliantly named Hercules
'Bumper' Wright. The game was arguably Leytham's finest
hour as he scored a scintillating hat-trick of tries. Indeed New
Zealand were so conscious of the threat he posed that they
withdrew strapping second row Bert Tyler from the pack
to mark him out wide. It didn't work: Jimmy's third effort
saw him outpace Bert and three other defenders down the
touchline before going round under the posts, Wigan won
12–8.

On the opposing team that day was Lance Todd and he was
to join with Leytham the following year as half of the historic
Wigan three-quarter line of Leytham, Bert Jenkins, Todd and
Joe Miller: a Lancastrian, a Welshman, a New Zealander and
a Wiganer. Revered throughout the game, spectators even
composed a not terribly good rhyme to immortalise the
fearsome foursome: 'Leytham, Jenkins, Miller and Todd: the
finest three-quarter line that ever did trod'.

Leytham led Wigan to their first League Championship
and enjoyed international success too, he was a member of
Great Britain's first touring team to Australia in 1910, scoring
four tries in the Brisbane Test, a feat that has still never been
matched against the Kangaroos. His career was effectively
ended by a nasty head injury sustained in a 1911 game against
Oldham and, after sharing a £330 benefit with Jim Sharrock
– Wigan's first – Jimmy died aged just 36 when he drowned
in a boating accident in Morecambe Bay on 20 August 1916.

**Appearances: 280 • Tries: 258 • Goals: 267 • Points: 1,308 •
Honours: League Championship 1909;
Lancashire Cup 1905, 1908, 1909;
Lancashire League Championship 1909, 1911, 1912;
South-West Lancashire League 1905, 1906**

MOST APPEARANCES FOR WIGAN

1	Jim Sullivan	774
2	Ken Gee	559
3	Ernie Ashcroft	530
4	Eric Ashton	497
5	Billy Boston	487
6	Shaun Edwards	467
7	Jack Cunliffe	447
8	Colin Clarke	436
9	Brian McTigue	422
10	Bill Francis	400
11	Bert Jenkins	389
12	Johnny Thomas	388
13	Andy Farrell	370

LEAGUE OF NATIONS

117 overseas players have played first-team rugby for Wigan. The total is made up of 46 Australians, 44 New Zealanders and the following luxury assortment:

Canada: Albert Cooper

Fiji: Kaiawa Bose

France: Jerome Guisset, Gael Tallec

Italy: Antonio Danielli, Tony Romano

Namibia: Andre Stoop

Papua New Guinea: Adrian Lam

Samoa: Shem Tatupu, Va'aiga Tuigamala

South Africa: David Booysen, Carl Burger, Nick du Toit, Tommy Gentles, Fred Griffiths, Rob Louw, Ray Mordt,

Fred Oliver, Constant van der Spuy, Attie van Heerden,
Nicholas van Heerden, George van Rooyen, Green Vigo
Tonga: Lee Hansen, Paul Koloi
Zimbabwe: Trevor Lake, John Winton

'THE WHITE HORSE FINAL'

Wigan 21 Oldham 4 (12 April 1924)

The 1923 FA Cup final between West Ham United and Bolton
Wanderers has passed into Wembley folklore as 'The White
Horse Final' due to the extraordinary scenes of mounted
policemen attempting to stem the vast crowds spilling
on to the pitch. Not quite so famous is the Rugby League
Challenge Cup final version which took place on the slightly
less hallowed turf of Rochdale's Athletic Ground just under a
year later. With two form teams making it to the showpiece, a
large gate was expected and sure enough, more than 41,000
paid to get in (already comfortably a record). Several thousand
more found their way into the ground gratis with many others
making use of the roof of the stands as a brave, if precarious,
vantage point. As kick-off approached, the crammed crowd
began pouring on to the pitch necessitating the use of police
horses to clear the playing area. After some doubt, the game
was allowed to proceed just a few minutes late with players
from both sides and the referee, the Revd Frank Chambers,
helping to get spectators back in position.

The throng continued to encroach during a tentative
opening where Oldham took a 2–0 lead from a penalty.
When Welsh second row Fred Roffey eventually rounded-
off a four-man Wigan move to score, the Cherry and Whites

were encouraged to open up. After 30 minutes they conjured one of the most famous tries in the game's history as Tommy Parker kicked on the turn and A.J. van Heerden won the race with his opposite number to collect, beat the full-back and dodge round a white horse standing guard in the in goal area before touching down under the posts. Play stopped for several minutes as the ecstatic crowd were moved back.

At half time, with Wigan 8–4 up, the worried Revd Chambers decided to turn around without a break for crowd safety reasons but several remarkable incidents continued to occur. At one point in the second half, van Heerden and an Oldham defender collided with a spectator who was on crutches, breaking one of them (the crutches, that is) and Wigan prop Bert Webster had a try disallowed just as he was plunging down amid a horse's hooves! As the half wore on, Wigan began to dominate; a superb Danny Hurcombe break led to Tommy Parker scoring in the corner, actually touching down 'at the feet of a young lady spectator' and then Tommy Howley sent Jack Price over, the speedy loose forward disappearing from view among the masses as he went in. Sullivan failed to convert either try from the touchlines – unsurprisingly, as he was virtually kicking from inside a crowd of people – but a Johnny Ring interception try, which Sullivan did goal, wrapped up a bizarre afternoon and won Wigan the Challenge Cup for the first time.

Wigan: Sullivan (3g), Ring (t), Howley, Parker (t), van Heerden (t), Jerram, Hurcombe, Webster, Banks, van Rooyen, Brown, Roffey (t), Price (t)

THE DOUBLE

The double of 20 tries and 100 goals in a single season has been achieved on four occasions but by only two Wigan players and, curiously, both men did it in consecutive seasons:

Colin Tyrer	1967/68	20 tries, 115 goals
Colin Tyrer	1968/69	21 tries, 126 goals
Pat Richards	2008	21 tries, 145 goals
Pat Richards	2009	23 tries, 102 goals

'THE BATTLE OF FARTOWN'

15 March 1981 was the date of one of the most notorious games in Wigan's history: a Second Division fixture against Huddersfield dubbed 'the Battle of Fartown'. Referee Vince Moss sent six players from the field during the second half, reducing the last 15 minutes of a dreadful match to a game of ten-a-side. The first 40 minutes was described as a 'running fight' with Wigan's Gary Stephens complaining he had been bitten and had skin studded off around his knee, while second row Steve O'Neill suffered painful after-effects from a violent smash to the mouth. About 5 minutes after the break, a 'general mêlée' saw the two stand-offs — Wigan's Les Bolton and Huddersfield's Glen Knight — red-carded, along with props Alan Hodkinson (Wigan) and Jim Johnson (Huddersfield). Another 10 minutes after that, Nicky Kiss and Huddersfield sub Steve Lyons headed for the showers too. Huddersfield won 9–7 in a game whose 'highlights' were shown on Granada TV. A Yorkshire radio commentator was criticised for describing the game as 'one for the connoisseur'.

PLAYER OF THE DECADE: 1910–20

Charles Seeling (1910–23)

Charlie 'Bronco' Seeling, Wigan's third Kiwi purchase after Lance Todd and 'Massa' Johnston, was clearly a forward ahead of his time. At 6ft and around 13½st, he was not only a big man by the standards of his day but possessed immense natural speed and stamina allied to a fearless defensive game. It was a rare mixture for the era and in the eleven Tests he played for the All Blacks Rugby Union team, he was already being lauded as one of their best ever forwards.

Rugby League scouts rarely ignored rave reviews of this sort and Wigan were said to have initially sniffed around Charlie during the All Blacks' 1905 British tour. They eventually got their man five years later, in January 1910, when he put pen to paper at the Dog & Partridge Hotel, Wallgate (now Last Orders). The directors described him as 'a golden nugget' and when, the following month, Seeling marked his debut with a try in a 67–0 hammering of Welsh club Merthyr, it looked like they had been right.

Over the next decade his storming displays from the loose forward berth played a major part in Wigan's success. In a time when forwards were expected to be very much the 'water carriers' for the glamorous backs, Seeling broke the mould by becoming a regular try-scorer. A great support player always ready to back up a break, he totalled 19 tries in his first full season (1910/11) – a then record for a forward at Wigan – which he surpassed with 22 in 1912/13. Having started out as a centre in his youth, his three-quarter's pace was a huge asset, enabling him frequently to charge across field and dispatch a speeding wing into touch when they assumed they had beaten the cover.

In January 1920, 'The Prince of Forwards' produced one of his most famous displays in a home league fixture with Barrow. The Cumbrians were leading 6–3 with barely 3 minutes to go and were anticipating their first ever win at Central Park, when Seeling took control, first powering over for a fine try and then from the restart, slicing straight through to put wing Harry Hall over for another.

Described as one of nature's gentlemen, Charlie was not only a great player but also an enthusiastic clubman and like many overseas players after him, he grew to love Wigan, settling in the town after retirement to run the Roebuck pub on Standishgate (now McDonalds). His son, Charlie Jr, also joined Wigan – from Warrington – in 1933 and played 86 games in the back row. In 1956, after forty-six years in the town, 73-year-old Charlie resolved to see out his final years in New Zealand and booked his passage home. Sadly he never made it, 12 days before he was due to sail, he and his wife and daughter were tragically killed in a car accident en route to see Charlie Jr at Dewsbury.

Appearances: 226 • Tries: 76 (plus 12 in wartime) •
Points: 228 (plus 36 in wartime) •
Honours: Lancashire Cup 1912; Lancashire League
Championship 1911, 1912, 1913, 1914, 1915

THE LANCE TODD TROPHY

The annual award for man of the match in the Challenge Cup final was named in memory of Wigan's first overseas player. Lance was a classy New Zealand centre who became a highly respected Salford coach and BBC summariser before his untimely death in a road accident in Oldham in 1942. Since its inauguration in 1946, the trophy has been won by a Wigan player on 14 occasions in their 23 final appearances: Cec Mountford (1951), Rees Thomas (1958), Brian McTigue (1959), Ray Ashby (1965)*, Brett Kenny (1985), Andy Gregory (1988 and 1990), Ellery Hanley (1989), Denis Betts (1991), Martin Offiah (1992 and 1994), Dean Bell (1993) Jason Robinson (1995) and Kris Radlinski (2002).

Sometime Wigan players who have won the award with other clubs are: Frank Collier, Eddie Cunningham, Joe Lydon, Henry Paul, Gary Connolly and Sean Long (3 times).

* jointly with Hunslet's Brian Gabbitas.

VOULEZ-VOUS UN PIE?

On 12 March 1947, Wigan entertained the French side Carcassonne at Central Park. It had snowed for several hours before kick-off and continued to do so with some ferocity during the match itself, yet the flamboyant visitors made light of the conditions to win 11—8. The fixture will chiefly be remembered for the antics of legendary French full-back Puig Aubert who, in addition to nonchalantly fielding a number of high balls one-handed while — legend has it — holding a lit cigarette in the other, accepted sips of coffee from people in the crowd and had the cheek to urinate in the centre of the pitch during the game. Must have been all that coffee. . . .

TEN GREAT: SPEEDSTERS

A perennial debate for rugby fans is the identity of the fastest ever player and, unless Usain Bolt ever fancies a run-out at The Willows on a Friday night, like all the best debates, there can never really be a definitive answer.

Wigan has a fine tradition of pace men, from the black and white days of the 'greyhound-like' Johnny Ring to the recent red and white blur that was Brett Dallas. 'Fastest ever' is, however, a hard term to define: some players — Jason Robinson perhaps — could beat anyone over the vital first 30m but were not possessed of the ability to hold off the most determined pursuers over the length of the pitch. Others — like Steve Renouf, a 10.7-second 100m man as a young Brisbane Bronco — appeared to have lost the electricity of youth by the time they pulled on the Cherry and White, and that's without considering factors such as change of pace, timing of run and footwork. All the same, for your next pub discussion, here are ten contenders based purely on what we know of their 100m times:

Martin Offiah (1992–7): The short-shorted, high-stepping showman is probably most people's automatic choice as our fastest ever and certainly few can have consistently produced such remarkable long-range tries against strong opposition. Offiah was clocked at 10.8 seconds for the 100m during his Widnes days, suggesting there have actually been quicker men in the Cherry and White, but perhaps none who quite possessed his anticipation, change of pace and priceless ability to transfer spike and track speed to boot and grass.

Mark Preston (1987–91): A clean-cut former England B Rugby Union flyer who paved the way for Offiah in an almost John the Baptist fashion, spoiling Central Park crowds with the expectation their left wing would routinely outpace everyone over long distances. A schoolboy athlete and regular clocker of 10.7 seconds for the 100m, his slender, dapper, almost 1920s appearance eventually led to John Monie deciding he could do without him and he went to Halifax in a £65,000 deal.

Gary Henley-Smith (1985): He may have had a funny name and a brief Wigan career – 7 matches including a Lancashire Cup final triumph – but he can make a strong claim to be the club's fastest wing. He was New Zealand national 100m and 200m champion in both 1982 and 1983 and has been credited with times of 10.4 seconds for the 100m and 21.4 seconds for the 200m.

Attie van Heerden (1923–6): The Springbok pin-up was crowned South African 120yd and 440yd hurdle champion in 1920 and competed in the 400yd hurdles in the Antwerp Olympics the same year.

Keri Jones (1968-71): A slim former Wales and British Lions Rugby Union star who clocked 21.8 seconds for the 220yds (as it then was) and reached the second round of both the 100yd and 220yd races at the 1966 Commonwealth Games in Kingston, Jamaica. He was also part of a Welsh 4 x 100 relay team whose national record time of 40.2 seconds stood for 30 years.

Paul Sampson (2004): The ex-Wakefield Trinity and England Rugby Union back won the 1996 England Schools 100m in a whirlwind time of 10.48 seconds. He didn't manage a first-team appearance during his short time at Wigan and his career – in both codes – has been badly affected by injury and ill luck. On the up side, he has had two sons with TV presenter Kirsty Gallacher.

Frank Carlton (1960–5): A sinewy former Saints wing and track athlete with a passion for Gilbert and Sullivan who bounced back from a serious leg injury to make an impression at Wigan. He was credited with around 10.9 seconds for the 100m.

Darren Williams (1993): Williams was a Cheshire sprint champion and English Schools 100m finalist who played only one first-team game. He was timed at 11 seconds dead for the 100m at the beginning of his brief Wigan career.

Brian Nordgren (1946–55): Described by his coach, Jim Sullivan, as the 'fastest thing on two legs', Nordgren was a suntanned, splendidly built lawyer who as well as being a New Zealand sprint champion was also a decent goalkicker.

Len Madden (1949): Introduced to the club by Johnny Ring, Madden played only 4 games for Wigan but managed to collect 8 tries including 4 against Wakefield. He was clearly a sprinter of some repute but stories that he once equalled the then British record of 9.7 seconds for 100yds don't appear to be backed-up by any official British athletic records.

TRANSFER FEES

Record Buys by Wigan:

Bill Hudson (back row) from Batley	£2,000	1947/48
Harry Street (loose forward) from Dewsbury	£5,000	1950/51
Mick Sullivan (wing) from Huddersfield	£9,500	1957/58
Ellery Hanley (stand-off/ loose forward) from Bradford	£85,000 cash (plus Steve Donlan and Phil Ford)	1985/86
Joe Lydon★ (utility back) from Widnes	£100,000	1986/87
Andy Gregory (scrum-half) from Warrington	£130,000	1986/87
Martin Offiah (wing) from Widnes	£440,000	1991/92
Stuart Fielden★ (prop) from Bradford	£450,000	2006

★ Record 'cash-only' fees, previous transfers involving cash and player exchange have totalled larger sums.

Record Sales by Wigan

Joe Egan (hooker) to Leigh	£5,000	1950/51
Mick Sullivan (wing) to St Helens	£11,000	1960/61
Bill Ashurst (back row) to Wakefield	£18,000	1977/78
George Fairbairn (full-back) to Hull KR	£72,500	1980/81
Ellery Hanley (loose forward) to Leeds	£250,000	1991/92

NB: Newcastle Falcons RUFC agreed to pay Wigan £750,000 for Va'aiga Tuigamala to switch codes in 1997. The payments were staggered over 5 years.

THE ST VALENTINE'S DAY MASSACRE

Wigan 116 Flimby & Fothergill 0 (14 February 1925)

In February 1925, Wigan drew Cumbrian amateurs Flimby & Fothergill United at home in the first round of the Challenge Cup. If their opponents sounded like a Dickensian law firm, they evidently played like one too, conceding 24 tries in a defeat that made their name a byword for defensive frailty. Welshmen Johnny Ring and Jim Sullivan had a field day, the former scoring a then club record 7 tries and the latter landing 22 goals, still a Rugby League record.

The visitors had arrived at Central Park claiming to be unbeaten all season with their try line crossed only once, but that proud record lasted barely a minute before Ring opened the scoring with a brilliant long-range try. He was swiftly followed over the line by jet-heeled Springbok Attie van Heerden, who collected 4 tries in the succeeding 14 minutes before switching off for the afternoon. There were later to be hat-tricks for captain Danny Hurcombe, South African scrum-half David Booysen and loose forward Jack Price.

The outclassed Flimby players grew so weary of trudging behind their posts while Sullivan booted over another 2 points that their winger, Robley, hid behind van Rooyen's bulk on the sideline before being spotted and reprimanded by the referee. When the score passed the 100-mark after Sullivan's conversion of Price's second try in the 67th minute, the scoreboard was unable to accommodate such a large number and had to use the first column of Flimby's part of the board. The game ended just short of Huddersfield's 119–2 defeat of Swinton Park Rangers in 1914, so Flimby & Fothergill went home to Cumbria with the consolation of not quite being the worst team ever and, with the compensatory share of the healthy 12,000 crowd's receipts, £520 richer.

Though we'd all like to think this record will be expunged by Wigan's first visit to St Helens' new stadium in 2011, in reality it is likely to stand for some considerable time and it deserves to: Wigan have come close to the score since — most recently in 2008 with a 106–8 victory over Whitehaven — but it should be remembered that tries were worth only 3 points in 1925, so in today's money, poor old Flimby & Fothergill were actually beaten 140–0.

Wigan: Sullivan (22g), Ring (7t), Howley (t), Hurcombe (3t), van Heerden (4t), Owens, Booysen (3t), Beetham (t), Banks, Burger, van Rooyen (2t), Roffey, Price (3t).

CRAZY NAMES, CRAZY GUYS

They registered plenty of points for Wigan but think what they might score in Scrabble:

VA'AIGA LEALUGA TUIGAMALA (1993–7)
IAFETA PALEAAESINA (2006–)
KAIAVA QASOTE BOSENAVULAGI (known as 'Kaia Bose') (1962)
CONSTANT WAHL VAN DER SPUY (1924)
LLEWELLYN LLEWELLYN (1912)

PLAYER OF THE DECADE: THE 1920s

Johnny Ring (1922–31)

A cursory glance at Johnny Ring's record is enough to explain why he ranks as one of the Wigan greats: he was simply a try-scoring phenomenon. Blessed with exceptional speed and evasive skills, he formed a remarkable understanding with his centre and fellow Welshman Tommy Howley. Howley realised the value of slipping his winger an early ball and the results, while a matter of record, are still scarcely believable. Ring's club record total of 62 tries in a season (1925/26) will probably never now be beaten and to average comfortably more than a try a game for over 300 matches is a staggering achievement.

A shunter at the Port Talbot steelworks during the week, Ring first showcased his try-scoring feats at Aberavon Rugby Union club, totalling 196 tries in 3 seasons including an incredible 76 in 1919/20. He was capped by Wales against England at Twickenham in 1921 (scoring a try, naturally) but joined Wigan for £800 in the summer of 1922. His sister was lame and one of the main reasons he gave for accepting League riches was to help her and, true to his word, he paid for a top surgeon to carry out the necessary operation shortly after his arrival at Central Park.

A talented footballer who played two seasons at centre forward for Swansea City, Johnny probably inherited his speed from his father, Cornelius Ring, a former Welsh sprint champion and he clearly put it to regular use in League, scoring 2 tries on his debut and going on to top the country's try charts in each of his first 4 seasons with his progressive totals of 41, 48, 52 and 62, thrice-breaking the club's tries in a season record. Johnny scored the final try in Wigan's 1924 'White Horse Final' Challenge Cup win and registered a hat-trick in the 1926 Championship Final. That game took place at Knowsley Road during the General Strike, and meant that with no public transport available, many Wigan fans simply walked to St Helens for the game. Ring and his team-mates felt they owed their supporters a performance after that. He also appeared in Wigan's win in the first Wembley showpiece, remarkably failing to mark the occasion with a try.

The top-scorer on the Great Britain tour to Australia and New Zealand in 1924, Ring was a modest and stylish individual who was hugely popular with the club's fans, yet when he reached 10 years' service, the board refused to grant him a benefit. The reason given was that he had signed for 'a considerable sum, possibly a record at the time and had been well rewarded since.' A disappointed Ring asked for a transfer and was listed at £100, going on to join Rochdale Hornets for a short spell. The directors came under immense criticism in the local press as a result. After his retirement, he qualified as a physiotherapist and masseur, staying in Wigan until his death in 1984.

**Appearances: 331 • Tries: 368 • Goals: 4 • Points: 1,112 •
Honours: League Championship 1926;
Challenge Cup 1924, 1929; Lancashire Cup 1922, 1928;
Lancashire League Championship 1923, 1924, 1926**

EARLY BATHS

On 29 October 1989, Steve Hampson achieved the distinction of being sent off twice in a weekend. On Saturday 28 October, in the second minute of the Test match at Headingley, he was sent packing for a head-butt on Kiwi scrum-half Gary Freeman – earning him the nickname 'Anchor' (the New

Zealand butter) – and the following afternoon he received his marching orders for a trip on Castleford's Australian full-back Steve Larder in a 20–22 league defeat at Central Park. A further sending-off in December against Leeds meant he totalled 14 games suspended during the 1989/90 season.

Wigan's first sending-off in the all-new Rugby League code seems to have occurred in a dour 0–5 away defeat to Tyldesley on 21 April 1896. Second row Elijah Prescott 'walked' along with his opposite number, Green, for what the *Wigan Observer* described as 'a bit of a tussle but nothing serious. There were no blows struck and a caution would have sufficed.' Perhaps Prescott had just become frustrated with what the same paper described as Tyldesley's 'fat, heavy forwards and clever half-backs who prefer to play a game of kicking into touch rather than good football.'

Surprisingly, the first Wigan player to be sin-binned was gentleman winger Dennis Ramsdale who was yellow-carded during a 31–12 victory away to Workington Town on 16 January 1983.

New Year's Day derbies with Warrington were always 'lively' and in 1988, a spectacularly bad-tempered affair resulted in a game of 11-a-side for an hour. Ten niggly minutes had elapsed when a huge brawl, sparked by a fight between Wigan prop Adrian Shelford and mad Australian Les Boyd, resulted in Shelford and Warrington's other prop, Tony Humphries, being red-carded. Boyd was sin-binned. After 20 minutes, Andy Goodway laid out Warrington's loquacious centre Paul Cullen with a late tackle and was sent off. As Goodway trudged away, the wronged Cullen, lying prone, suddenly sprang up and chased him, launching himself at the departing loose forward with a flurry of punches. His moment of madness began another mass punch-up and saw him sent off too, probably costing Warrington the chance of victory as the match ended 15 all.

Mistaken identity was commonplace in the mid-1980s when Rugby League teams tended to be amorphous masses of facial hair and mud. As a result, New Year's Day 1986 saw Nicky Kiss suffering a miscarriage of justice (for once) when he was sent off for a high shot when the real culprit had been Shaun Wane. In a game at Leigh in February 1982, Glyn Shaw was so annoyed to have been sent off for a 'misjudgement' by Danny Campbell that he resolved to shave off the *de rigueur* Wigan pack beard.

BROTHERS IN ARMS

Brothers who have played for Wigan's first team:
Billy and Jack Blan
Bill and Frank Collier
James and Thomas Coyle
A. Duffy and H. Duffy
Cliff and David Hill
Kevin and Tony Iro
Keiron and Kevin O'Loughlin
Ted and Vince Smith
Joel and Sam Tomkins
Attie and Nicholas van Heerden
Mark and Peter Vickers
Joe and John Winstanley

MEN OF STEEL

The award for the season's outstanding player in the British game was begun by Manchester-based Trumanns Steel in 1977. Wigan winners of the main prize are: George Fairbairn (1980), Ellery Hanley (1987 and 1989), Shaun Edwards (1990), Dean Bell (1992), Andy Platt (1993), Denis Betts (1995) and Andy Farrell (1996 and 2004).

Doug Laughton, Joe Lydon, Ellery Hanley, Martin Offiah and Sean Long are all sometime Wigan players who have picked up the award but not when playing for the Cherry and Whites.

THE FIRST WEMBLEY

Wigan 13 Dewsbury 2 (4 May 1929)

Wigan are a club who like to do the 'firsts' in Rugby League, so looking back, it seems unsurprising that such a major event as the first fixture at 'The Empire Stadium' should feature the Cherry and Whites but, in reality, this is probably where their pioneering reputation came from. Fans of both sides were desperate to make the journey south despite the 10s 6d Wigan to London train fare being quite a sacrifice in the economically barren 1920s. A Wigan miner called H.H. Townend walked all the way to Wembley clad in one of Jim Sullivan's old jerseys with a card reading 'Rugby Cup Final. Wigan v Dewsbury. I am walking from Wigan to Wembley'.

Wigan's preparation consisted of bracing walks up to Parbold Hill or through Haigh Plantations with the odd run around a field or game of golf. Their dazzling backs were expected to run riot in the open space, but Dewsbury promised their mighty forwards and teamwork would cause an upset. Such was the sense of occasion, several VIPs and politicians were enticed to attend. Greenall's brewery magnate Lord Daresbury was on hand to present the silverware and the Revd Frank Chambers provided commentary for BBC Radio. Wigan had struggled through to the final – requiring replays in the third round and semi-final and on the day itself nerves began to build. The players even got lost several times in the tunnels leading to the pitch *Spinal Tap*-style. Even so, Wigan can claim to be the first side on to the field and first to kick off at Wembley.

It was inevitably Jim Sullivan who registered the first Rugby League points at the stadium after just 3 minutes with a penalty for offside. Dewsbury lost their centre Herbert Hirst with a fractured rib, meaning in the days before subs, Wigan enjoyed a numerical advantage. Just after his departure, the first try followed when Wigan stand-off Syd Abram raced in. Dewsbury full-back Jack Davies yanked the Yorkshiremen into the game with a spectacular drop goal from his own half that sparked a concerted period of pressure for Wigan's opponents either side of half time, but Wigan's defence held firm and, as the game wore on, the class of their backs eventually told. Scottish centre Roy Kinnear – father of the late film actor of the same name – took charge, creating one try, before scoring another under the posts in the 70th minute that Sullivan converted. The Welsh full-back then became the very first Rugby League player to climb the 39 steps and receive the Challenge Cup at Wembley.

Wigan: Sullivan (2g), Ring, Parker, Kinnear (t), Brown (t), Abram (t), Binks, Hodder, Bennett, Beetham, Stephens, Mason, Sherrington

CLUB MASCOTS

Like their half-backs, since the advent of Super League, Wigan have seen fit to employ a number of mascots, with some proving better than others:

1998: The Edwards Pie Man (a fondly remembered smiley pie with legs)

1999: Winston the Warrior (alarming looking long-haired warrior thing)

2000: Kelvin the Gorilla (large African mountain gorilla named in honour of one of the club's most combative props. Seems to be back at the club in an advisory capacity to Max)

2003–: Max the Warrior (popular, silver-helmeted character with a more child-friendly countenance than the nightmarish Winston)

SHEEP STOPS PLAY

Canine pitch invasions have always been part of Rugby League, but in December 1923 the Wigan versus Broughton Rangers fixture at Central Park was interrupted by the mysterious appearance of a sheep on the playing area. According to the *Wigan Observer*, play was held up for several minutes while 'two police officers made futile attempts to catch the animal.' In the end it fell to the Welsh duo of Johnny Ring and 'Dodger' Owens to utilise all their speed and skill to collar the animal and remove it from the field.

IF YOU WANT TO PLAY FOR WIGAN
No. I: BILLY JONES

Desperate to give your son every chance of playing for Wigan one day? Then try to ensure your surname is Jones and you christen him with some variation on the name William. Fifty-six Bills, Billys, Willies and Williams have played first-team rugby for the club making it – just – the most common Christian name. Sixteen Joneses have worn the Cherry and White, making it comfortably the most common surname. However, the only player so far to actually combine both, centre Bill Jones, enjoyed a modest Wigan career. He played just 7 tryless games in 1901 after being bought from Swinton.

TEN GREAT:
TRIES AGAINST SAINTS

Obviously, all tries against Saints are great tries and there are at least 20 more worthy of making this list, but here are just 10:

26 December 1908, Jack Prescott
(Saints 7 Wigan 22 at Knowsley Road)

Superstar Jim Leytham was Wigan's main man in this convincing Boxing Day victory with another hat-trick and 2 goals but the score of the match came from scrum-half Prescott, who according to the *Wigan Observer*, scored in 'a remarkable manner'. In the dying minutes he 'picked up with surprising skill when travelling at high speed, dashed through the opposing players and, when seemingly tackled, he put them off the scent with a feigned pass. Then he again got into his stride and completed a beautiful try under the posts.'

9 March 1957, Norman Cherrington
(Saints 11 Wigan 20 at Knowsley Road)

From the earliest days of Coldrick and Seeling to modern thoroughbreds such as Betts and Goodway, Wigan have always prized free-running forwards and Norman Cherrington may just have been the quickest of the lot. A schoolboy sprint star with Leigh Harriers and one of the first players to experiment with – then abandon – contact lenses, he demonstrated his athleticism with a stunning effort in this rearranged Boxing Day fixture. Collecting the ball on his own 25, he appeared to have taken the wrong option in the wet conditions by simply hoofing the ball ahead and setting off in pursuit, yet he followed at such remarkable pace he was able to collect the initial favourable bounce and race round under the posts for one of the great forward tries.

20 April 1962, Frank Carlton
(Saints 16 Wigan 18 at Knowsley Road)

In a thrilling, see-saw Good Friday fixture featuring some world-class running from Tom van Vollenhoven, Wigan came back from 11–4 down to seal victory with a sensational late try: stand-off Dave Bolton found Carlton 60yds out and the Saints-born flyer bamboozled three defenders before skinning full-back Keith Northey for a classic score.

28 April 1962, Eric Ashton
(Wigan 12 Saints 3 at Central Park)

In a game already illuminated by a great 50yd score from Wigan loose forward Geoff Lyon, this was a wonderful effort, sparked by full-back 'Punchy' Griffiths 80yds out, the move continued with scrum-half Frankie Parr and was finished with his customary elan by St Helens-born Wigan skipper Eric Ashton.

3 March 1990, Andy Goodway
(Saints 14 Wigan 20 at Old Trafford)

Saints had gone down 27–0 in the previous year's Challenge Cup final and, determined to make amends under new coach Mike McClennan, had produced a spirited semi-final display to push an out-of-sorts Wigan all the way. With less than 4 minutes to go, the scores were locked at 14 all and at least a replay looked to be their just reward when the mighty Ellery Hanley summoned something extra from his weary body, weaved past 2 defenders and handed on to the supporting Andy Goodway to break Saints hearts and send 'The Riversiders' to a third successive Wembley.

26 December 1990, Frano Botica
(Saints 15 Wigan 28 at Knowsley Road)

Frano Botica could patently kick goals but halfway through his debut season, Wigan fans still had plenty of doubts about the wiry, defensively frail unknown from Rugby Union. At least, they did until he scored the first try in a blood-and-thunder Boxing Day fixture. Playing on the left wing, he picked up a kick right in the corner on his own try line, curved across field past 5 defenders, offloaded to Kevin Iro, looped round to take the return pass and then held off frantic Saints chasers for a length-of-the-field score that probably covered 125yds in total. 'He'll do, yon mon.'

26 December 1994, Va'aiga Tuigamala
(Saints 25 Wigan 32 at Knowsley Road)

This was the moment 'Inga' sealed his status as a crowd favourite. Wigan had been comfortably leading this game early on before the referee (and, I suppose you have to say, grudgingly, some fine play from Saints halves Goulding and Martyn) fashioned a barnstorming comeback to put the home side in the lead. Henry Paul had been harshly sent off in the first half and trips to the sin bin for Skerrett, Connolly and Cowie meant Wigan played much of the second period with 11 men; unsurprisingly Saints had made this advantage tell and looked to have snatched the points. Then, with 4 minutes left on the clock, Tuigamala collected a pass from Connolly and with nothing looking on, simply straightened his run and rampaged through four tackles to score his second try of the match: one of the very greatest moments from an era full of them.

14 April 1995, Henry Paul
(Wigan 34 St Helens 18 at Central Park)

The Wigan side of this period made a habit of doing things you never thought you'd see and one of their chief magicians was the sparkling Kiwi Henry Paul. The full-back had already scored one mouth-watering try with a first-half surge and, as Wigan marched towards the League Champions' party that the final whistle would herald, he conjured a second that still beggars belief. Wigan were forced to drop out from under their own posts and teenage giant Andy Farrell did the honours, lofting a typical effort some 50m upfield. Saints forwards Sonny Nickle and Ian Pickavance allowed the ball to bounce as normal without realising that Paul was chasing the kick as he had everything that afternoon like some sort of guided missile. The Saints players had barely registered contact between ball and grass when Paul blurred between them, gathering it in flypaper hands and cantering on for the remaining 50m to the posts eventually slowing to a gentle, mocking stroll.

5 September 2003, Brian Carney
(Saints 4 Wigan 28 at Knowsley Road)

Probably the third best try of the Irishman's *annus mirablilis*. Fielding a kick on his own 10m line, Carney burst through the first line of defence and hared 90m up the right wing to score his second try of the match in the corner. The sight of an emotional Mike Gregory in the stands triumphantly punching the air became an iconic image for Wigan fans.

14 September 2007, David Vaealiki
(Wigan 20 St Helens 12 at the JJB Stadium)

This try's inclusion is less to do with its quality – though it was a good one – than the fact it was such a surprise. The scorer, David Vaealiki, had arrived at Wigan on big money trumpeted as 'the new Kevin Iro'. He had been an outstanding junior player and was a popular part of the Parramatta squad in the NRL, but it quickly became obvious he had been badly blunted by an Achilles injury and he was to become a byword for the club's expensive underachievers of the Super League era. In this, his final home game for Wigan, he took Sean O'Loughlin's pass and raced 75yds down the left wing, dummying to supporting team-mates before accelerating away from a shell-shocked Paul Wellens to score. It was – finally – a glimpse of what we all hoped for in his previous 71 outings and if applause was muted it wasn't for reasons of maliciousness, it was just that the home crowd were too busy rubbing their eyes.

BALLS IN BAGS

On Monday 3 January 1972, Wigan were fairly satisfied to be drawn at home to Salford in the first round of the Challenge Cup. However, neighbours Leigh immediately registered an official complaint after noticing their ball had dropped from the bag before the end of the live televised draw, resulting in their being left with the unappealing prospect of a trip to Headingley to face Leeds.

A redraw was held on Thursday 6 January giving the Leythers a more palatable home fixture with Workington and again pairing Wigan with Salford, only this time . . . away. For the record, Wigan won 16–12 before going out at Wakefield Trinity in round two.

On Monday 2 December 1985, Wigan found themselves in the bag for another TV draw, this time for the JPS Trophy quarter-finals. Their number came out first, followed by Barrow, no doubt perfectly acceptable save for the fact 'The Shipbuilders' had actually been knocked out in the previous round. Red-faced officials suggested the stray ball must have been lodged in the lining and continued on, pulling out Leigh to make the short trip to Central Park. However, when the penultimate team, York, was announced, there appeared to be no ball for the last team, Hull!

When the inevitable second draw was made, Wigan were presented with the much stiffer task of Warrington away. Happily, they won 26–22 and went on to lift the trophy that year.

PLAYER OF THE DECADE: THE 1930s

James Sullivan (1921–46)

Boston might have been more exciting, Hanley might have been more mysteriously charismatic and Edwards might have been from Wigan, but if you add ability to longevity and throw in coaching record, then it is very difficult to look past James Kevin Sullivan as Wigan's greatest-ever signing. 'Peerless Jim' was unarguably the finest goal-kicker in the club's history but his tackling, strong running and tactical brain mark him out as a complete one-off. In his long, distinguished career he came to embody his club in a way that no one had before or since.

Sullivan was only a slender 17-year-old Cardiff RUFC player when, in 1921, he became the youngest player to be selected for the Barbarians, leading to press predictions that a future Welsh icon had been unearthed. However, five Rugby League clubs were already interested in him, Wigan deciding to make a move after Sullivan had impressed their scouts who were in Cardiff to watch another player. As an apprentice boilermaker with little prospect of work, Jim was happy to accept Wigan's 12-year £750 contract in June 1921 and began an extraordinary 31-year association with the club.

Hoping to ease his way into the new game in the 'A' team, he was bluntly told he hadn't been expensively brought north to play for the reserves and made his debut against Widnes in front of a curious but expectant crowd in August and, despite some mistakes and shock at the pace of the game, he kicked five goals in a 21–0 win. It was the beginning of a remarkable career of point-accumulation and trophy-collection; Sullivan soon became the dominant personality in the world game and opposing teams were obsessed with stopping him. One rival club were even alleged to have put two bladders into a doctored match ball to sabotage his metronomic kicking. After landing a staggering 172 goals in his second season he was rewarded with a silver rose bowl from the delighted supporters, and a gold pocket watch and miniature gold rugby ball from the directors. Jim practiced his kicking constantly from being a schoolboy and as well as accuracy, possessed a booming boot capable of landing long distance.

A big man for the time, he was described as 'The Rugby League Carnera' after Primo Carnera, the Italian man-mountain who was World Heavyweight Boxing champion in the 1930s. Opposing fans derided Sullivan as slow, but no one could actually ever recall seeing him outpaced and he was a close second behind Sid Jerram in a 100yd sprint race before the first ever Wigan Sevens. As a player he commanded enormous respect in both hemispheres, and as a very successful coach, who ironically propounded a 'Thou Shalt Not Kick' philosophy when in charge, he if anything increased the esteem in which he was held. Jim spent 56 years of his life in Wigan and his death in 1977 was mourned like the loss of a monarch.

Appearances: 774 • Tries: 83 • Goals: 2,317 •
Points: 4,883 • Honours: RL Championship 1922, 1926,
1934; Challenge Cup 1924, 1929;
Lancashire Cup 1922, 1928, 1938;
Lancashire League Championship 1923, 1924, 1926

TOP GOAL-SCORERS FOR WIGAN

1	Jim Sullivan	2,317
2	Andy Farrell	1,335
3	Frano Botica	840
4	Colin Tyrer	813
5	Fred Griffiths	663
6	George Fairbairn	594
7	Ken Gee	508
8	Ted Ward	480
9	Eric Ashton	448
10	Johnny Thomas	439
11	Colin Whitfield	392
12	Laurie Gilfedder	384
13	Jack Cunliffe	371

WIGAN AND FRIENDS

The 1992 Great Britain tour to Australia saw Wigan supply an astonishing 13 players to the squad: Denis Betts, Phil Clarke, Neil Cowie, Martin Dermott, Shaun Edwards, Andy Gregory, Steve Hampson, Ian Lucas, Joe Lydon, Billy McGinty, Martin Offiah, Andy Platt and Kelvin Skerrett. A fourteenth, Dave Myers, was later flown over to Australia as a replacement. In the 33–10 second Test win in Melbourne, Wigan provided all 6 starting forwards, the first time a club had done this.

The previous record of 8 tourists was also achieved by Wigan when Ernie Ashcroft, Tommy Bradshaw, Jack Cunliffe, Joe Egan, Ken Gee, Jack Hilton, Gordon Ratcliffe and Martin Ryan set sail for Australia in 1950.

HAT-TRICKS

Up to the end of the 2009 season, 728 hat-tricks had been scored for the Wigan first team. The following players achieved the feat on 10 or more occasions:

	TOTAL	3t	4t	5t	6t	7t	10t
Billy Boston	51	35	11	1	2	2	-
Johnny Ring	38	24	5	4	2	3	-
Brian Nordgren	37	27	7	3	-	-	-
Jimmy Leytham	27	24	2	-	1	-	-
Martin Offiah	23	15	3	4	-	-	1
Jack Morley	22	12	8	2	-	-	-
Gordon Ratcliffe	17	9	6	-	1	1	-
Ellery Hanley	16	9	5	1	1	-	-
Trevor Lake	14	9	5	-	-	-	-
Johnny Lawrenson	14	10	3	1	-	-	-
Jack Hilton	13	8	4	1	-	-	-
Johnny Miller	13	8	4	1	-	-	-
Alf Ellaby	12	8	3	1	-	-	-
Ernie Ashcroft	11	9	2	-	-	-	-
Lewis Bradley	11	7	2	1	1	-	-
Jason Robinson	11	10	-	1	-	-	-
Eric Ashton	10	8	1	1	-	-	-
Shaun Edwards	10	4	5	-	-	-	1

Wigan's first Rugby League hat-trick was scored by Cumbrian centre John Timoney in a 28–3 Challenge Cup first-round victory over a team called Groves United at the old Prescott Street ground on 18 March 1899.

On 19 October 1912, Stewart's the King Tailors – a nationwide chain – decided to increase their successful football 'Overcoats for Goals' promotion into Rugby League. Their Wallgate branch confidently promised 'one of our famous Sovereign overcoats to any Wigan player who scores three tries in any Northern Union league match played at home. In addition, we will give an extra coat to any spectator each successful player brings with him.' The next home game saw Wigan beat Coventry 70–0 thanks to 4 tries from Lew Bradley and further trebles for Lance Todd, Dick Ramsdale and Robert Curwen. Three days later Bradley and Curwen scored 3 each again in a 41–4 defeat of Runcorn, leading Stewart's to hurriedly reconsider their promotion (presumably before they went bust).

Arguably Wigan's finest quality hat-trick was scored by South African speedster Green Vigo on 22 October 1977 in a televised first-round John Player tie against Leeds at Headingley. In a thrilling 25–22 win – also containing great tries from the Jimmys Hornby and Nulty – the former fisherman displayed such devastating running ability that his opposite number, Leeds legend John Atkinson, concluded that it might just be time for him to retire. The first saw Vigo receive the ball around 65yds out, take Atkinson on the outside, beat another defender with a classic in and out and despite being ankle-tapped, get up to use his strength to carry three tacklers over the line. The second and third were almost carbon-copy 50m efforts as he outpaced Atkinson on the outside, feinted in and out to beat the full-back, before running round to touch down and celebrate with his trademark 'blowing kisses' celebration. Each one of his 3 tries was considered good enough to appear in the BBC's seminal 1989 VHS release, *101 Rugby League Tries*.

On 13 November 1988, Wigan thrashed a depleted Runcorn Highfield 92–2 in a John Player Trophy first-round tie at Central Park. Kevin Iro (4) and Tony Iro (3) became the first brothers to score hat-tricks in the same match for Wigan. Kevin also kicked 9 goals for a personal haul of 34 points.

Seven Wigan players have scored hat-tricks on their first-team debuts, coincidentally all in home games. Here they are:

James Rynn (3) v Dewsbury	2 April 1923	League
Gordon Innes (3) v Hunslet	16 September 1933	League
Alf Ellaby (3) v Oldham	25 August 1934	League
Terry O'Grady (3) v Whitehaven	2 February 1957	League
Dave Willicombe (3) v Castleford Lock Lane	2 February 1974	Challenge Cup R1
Stuart Turner (3) v Keighley	24 November 1991	Regal Trophy R2
Sam Tomkins (5) v Whitehaven	12 May 2008	Challenge Cup R5★

★ Sam Tomkins scored his first 3 tries in the opening 12 minutes of his debut, surely also Wigan's quickest debut hat-trick and equal with Attie van Heerden's 3 in the first 12 minutes of the famous Flimby & Fothergill fixture in 1925.

'FOOTBALL IN THE FOG'

Boxing Day 1938 saw Wigan entertain Salford at Central Park. The visitors were coached by Lance Todd and captained by the legendary Gus Risman, so Wigan fans had every right to expect to see a memorable encounter and they were half right. At kick-off time, the ground suddenly became shrouded in thick fog, described by contemporary reports as 'almost a complete blackout'. The *Wigan Observer* correspondent remarked, 'It was hardly possible for someone standing at the foot of one set of posts to discern the other set up the field.'

Financially, Wigan needed the game to proceed and even though many of the 8,000 crowd felt it should have been postponed, they apparently took proceedings in 'good humoured Christmas spirit'. Despite not even being able to make out the Popular Stand directly across from the press box, the *Observer* reporter of the time produced a superb match report, describing players 'alternately appearing and disappearing' in fog and concluding 'Salford apparently won this match on their merits', conceding that at least in the scrums visible to the press box, they seemed to be on top. At one point, Salford forward Dalton scored, unbeknownst to the press until their wing Barney Hudson obligingly came over to the touchline and shouted the news up to reporters. Wigan were defeated 11–0, as the paper put it: 'The worst match the crowd never saw at Central Park.'

PLAYER OF THE DECADE: THE 1940s

Joe Egan (1938–50)

Will we ever again see a hooker moving between two clubs for the Rugby League record transfer fee as Joe Egan did in 1950? It was a mark of how far ahead of his time Egan was. One of the greatest products of Wigan St Patrick's ARLFC, a club that has many a contender for that accolade, he joined Wigan for £25 at the age of 17 in 1937. Joe was initially a full-back but was converted into a hooker by the time he made his first-team bow away at Leigh in October 1938, and while he proved to be perfectly adept in the art of winning scrums, he differed from the traditional rake in his rare ability with ball in hand.

Egan formed a menacing partnership with prop Ken Gee and, illustrating a fine rugby brain and leadership qualities, he became club captain during the club's wartime fixtures. As a brass moulder by trade, he had a 'reserved occupation' during the conflict which meant he was able to stay at home, play for Wigan and be part of the Home Guard, though some in the town frowned on him, thinking he was 'dodging the war'. He nevertheless has fond memories of the period as local lads pitched in to cover absentee players and became part of the Wigan side still continuing to bring success.

Joe retained the captaincy after the war, allowing him to become the first player to receive the Challenge Cup from royalty when King George VI attended Wembley in 1948. Twice a Great Britain tourist and once captain, he missed Wigan's 1946 and 1950 Championship Final victories due to being at sea with Great Britain heading to Australia, but won plenty more and changed the face of the hooking role with his ball-playing ability and supporting work rate. Joe was 31 when he secured his record transfer down the road to Leigh as player-coach and though his glittering playing career was effectively ended by a broken leg in 1953, he continued to coach and returned to Central Park in that capacity in 1956, the first Wiganer to be appointed to the position. He brought more success to the club before departing after the Wembley defeat by St Helens in 1961. He wrote on Rugby League for the *Daily Express* and the *Wigan Evening Post* and, at 91, still lives in Wigan to this day.

Appearances: 362 • Tries: 28 • Goals: 12 • Points: 108 • Honours: League Championship 1944, 1946, 1947, 1950; Challenge Cup 1948; Lancashire Cup 1938, 1946, 1947, 1948, 1949; Lancashire League Championship 1946, 1947, 1950

HARRY SUNDERLAND TROPHY

The award for man of the match in the Championship, Premiership and now Grand Final is named after a respected Australian administrator who was once Wigan's manager. It has been awarded every year since 1965, the year after Harry's death, and it is a reflection of Wigan's concentration on the Challenge Cup over the years that of the 45 times it has been handed out, on only 8 occasions has it gone to a Wigan player: Bill Ashurst (1971), Joe Lydon (1987), Andy Platt (1992), Sam Panapa (1994), Kris Radlinski (1995), Andy Farrell (1996 and 1997) and Jason Robinson (1998).

Sometime Wigan players who have won it with other clubs are: Terry Fogerty, Mal Aspey, Henry Paul, Paul Deacon and Michael Withers.

NICKNAMES

Paul 'Patch' Atcheson

Dean 'Mean Dean' Bell

George 'Darkie' Bennett (clearly less enlightened times!)

George 'Chicken George' Carmont (worked in a chicken factory)

Colin 'Curly' Clarke

Gary 'Lager' Connolly

Jack 'Gentleman Jack' Cunliffe

Peter 'Iron Man' Davies

Greg 'The Wall' and 'Dish Head' Dowling

Nick 'Rambo' du Toit

Shaun 'Gizmo' Edwards (a character from the film *Gremlins* he supposedly resembles)

Steve 'The Zip Zip Man' Ella

Jimmy 'Jinking Jimmy' Fairhurst

John 'Chicka' Ferguson

Arthur 'Bolla' Francis

Wayne 'Wagga' Godwin

Andy 'BA' Goodway

Fred 'Punchy' Griffiths

Ellery 'The Black Pearl' Hanley

Jack 'The Flying Saucer' Hilton

Kevin 'The Beast' Iro

Bill 'Massa' Johnston

Denzil 'Cowboy' Jones

Jack 'Safety Pin' Mason (he held everything together at the back)

Len 'The Baby' Mason

Cec 'The Blackball Bullet' Mountford (he was fast and err ... from Blackball)

David 'Doc' Murray

Augustine 'Ducky' O'Donnell (schoolboy nickname from Donnell Duck)

Martin 'Chariots' Offiah (and yes, we know it's really pronounced 'Offeeyer')

George 'Dodger' Owens

Iafeta 'Feka' Paleaaesina (commentators Down Under tried to saddle him with 'Mr Effective' which sounds like a cleaning product)

Mark 'Bond' Preston a.k.a. 'The Preston Express'

Scott 'Foo' Quinnell (say it quickly!)

Gordon 'Spider' Ratcliffe (he was all arms and legs)

Rhys 'The Flying Barber' Rees

Steve 'The Pearl' Renouf

Jason 'Billy Whizz' Robinson (later appeared alongside his namesake in the *Beano*)

Mark 'Piggy' Riddell

Bill 'Soss' Sayer

Green 'The Saldhana Tiger' Vigo

Graeme 'Tex' West

TEN GREAT: HARD MEN

Clearly all Rugby League players are hard men and, like the fastest man debate, everyone will have their personal favourite, but here are just some of those you wouldn't want to irritate in a King Street kebab shop queue in the early hours:

Jeremiah Shea (1921–4) At 5ft 8in and just over 11st, Welsh docker 'Jerry' Shea was certainly not the biggest centre to have played for Wigan but he might just have been the toughest. Jim Sullivan, who watched Wigan until he died in 1977, said he'd never seen a modern centre capable of living with him. A professional boxer, Shea was renowned for his punching power and won many notable bouts, as well as losing only narrowly to world welterweight champion Ted 'Kid' Lewis. He was also a high-class professional middle-distance runner and a talented swimmer who once rescued a drowning child from the treacherous waters of the River Usk.

In 1920, playing for Wales Rugby Union against England, Jerry became the first person to score a full house (try, conversion, penalty and drop goal) in an international match, but his selfish and disruptive personality meant he was an unpopular figure in the squad and as such, a natural candidate for tempting north. A record £700 signing on Christmas Day 1921, he typically refused to ever move to Wigan, preferring to travel up from Newport for games and certainly there was no one in Wigan brave enough to tell him that was wrong. Hard and intimidating he may have been, but he was a lavishly gifted footballer too, and his superb match-winning long-distance try in the 1922 Championship Final against Oldham – jinking and stepping past three defenders – will go down as one of Wigan's finest.

George van Rooyen (1923–8) He was a strapping South African with Marvel comic strength who was the pack enforcer in the days of 'anything goes'. In one game against St Helens Recs he ripped his cheek to such an extent he was able to poke his tongue through it, but refused to go off as he didn't want the opposition to know they could hurt him. Legend has it he once laid out a persistently niggling player with one punch, turned to the referee and said calmly 'The name is van Rooyen' before walking off.

Brian McTigue (1950–66) 'The Quiet Man' epitomised old-fashioned League prop chic with his broken nose, damaged teeth and coal mine-honed physique, but for all his toughness – and he was very tough – McTigue was a runner and handler of rare talent. Previously a very competent cruiserweight boxer featuring in over 50 professional fights, he was good enough to be offered the chance to box in the USA after impressing world champion Joey Maxim during an exhibition bout. Thankfully he stuck to Rugby League and became a Wigan great. Possessed of remarkable ball skills – honed by a love of basketball dating from his National Service – his strength and toughness terrified the Australians. In a Test match at the SCG, he famously once used his considerable pugilistic skill to subdue Aussie tough guy Norm Provan, knocking the massive Kangaroo second row cold with an almost imperceptible movement of the fist. McTigue said later he felt ashamed of the punch, but it earned him even greater respect Down Under.

Mick Sullivan (1957–60) The most capped Great Britain international of all time may have only been a 5ft 10in and 13st winger, but Sullivan could match even the biggest forwards for aggressive attitude and ferocious tackling. In the 1958 Challenge Cup final, he laid out Workington stand-off Harry Archer so forcefully that Archer complained of headaches for months. As a winger who thrived on defence, Sullivan's trademark bone-crunching crash tackles and desire to constantly test the mental strength of his opponent made him a hate figure for rival fans who routinely threw abuse and occasionally missiles at him as he prowled the touchline. He missed the 1960 Championship Final after fighting with Alex Murphy in the semi and was famously one of 6 men sent off – 2 forwards and all 4 wingers – in GB's bloodbath encounter with New South Wales at the SCG in 1962. Always a controversial figure, he appeared in a Sunday newspaper in 1970 threatening to 'blow the lid off Rugby League' and is proud to have been twice banned *sine die* by the Rugby League authorities.

Kurt Sorensen (1976–7) The squat Kiwi's pantomime villain reputation was predominantly forged at Widnes, but his first British club was Wigan and the coach of the time, legendary hard man Vince Karalius, saw enough of the curly-haired hit man to be desperate to get him back the following season. Packing 16st into a height of around 5ft 9in, Sorensen made his debut for Auckland's Mount Wellington club aged just 15, an illustration of the inherent hardness of his Tongan and Danish ancestors. He was very speedy for a prop but was best known for his deliberately cultivated 'animal' reputation and for never taking a backward step.

Glyndwyr Shaw (1981–4) A granite-tough former coal miner and Welsh Rugby Union prop standing 6ft 2in and weighing more than 15st, 'Glyn' stiffened the Wigan pack of the early 1980s after a £30,000 move from Naughton Park. A powerful scrummager and straight runner, seemingly always sporting a headband and gnarled expression, he is the subject of many oft-told stories, some no doubt true, many not. Reputed to have once played the ball with a broken leg at Central Park, run straight through a closed door and to have spent an evening at Neath Rugby Club opening beer bottles with his teeth after the bar's opener broke, his career at Wigan was short in time but long on commitment and respect.

Greg Dowling (1985–6) Dowling was a strapping Aussie prop known as 'The Wall' for his impenetrability and 'Dish Head' because of the concave nature of his frequently struck face. He made only 25 appearances in the Cherry and White but these included conspicuous displays in the Lancashire Cup and John Player Trophy final victories and Wigan badly missed his steel when he returned to Australia. Footage of his famous 1985 Brisbane Test match brawl with New Zealand's Kevin Tamati where the pair continued to exchange blows on the sidelines after having been sent off is still an internet favourite to this day. Greg now runs a McDonalds restaurant in North Queensland where, I imagine, not many people come in to use his toilet without ordering food.

Les Davidson (1990) Davidson was a big, nasty Aussie Test prop who was a short-term signing (11 matches) to cover for 1990 New Zealand tourist Adrian Shelford. With the South Sydney Rabbitohs and Cronulla Sharks, Les carved out a reputation as of one the most ruthless and intimidating front-rowers in the NRL with a penchant for knocking opponents out cold. In 1994, playing for the Sharks against St George he was sent off after knocking out three opponents with three punches. He also played a large number of matches with a detached retina, shrugging off the handicap by asking team mates to help him get into the defensive line.

Kelvin Skerrett (1990–6) Skerrett was an almost caricature front-row forward of the old school: barrel-chested, stubble-chinned and hard as nails. It is surprising to learn that Kelvin – nephew of another GB prop Trevor Skerrett – was only sent off on four occasions during his Wigan career, though he sailed close to the wind in most of his games and the supporters loved him for it. His hilarious, playing to the stalls body language when called out for a misdemeanour were great sport for both sets of fans and while his rampaging style occasionally cost club and player dearly – he missed the 1991 Cup final and Championship decider through suspension – he provided the necessary darker dimension to Wigan's dazzling big-match teams. Enjoying run-ins with all the notable pack stars of his era, he is probably best remembered for his spectacular intervention in a Challenge Cup quarter-final brawl with Featherstone at Central Park in 1994 when he soared through the air to land on top of a goal line mêlée, an act he claims was merely 'peacemaking'. It earned him the nickname 'Super Kel'.

Quentin Pongia (2003–4) Pongia was a grey-haired, grizzled front-row veteran from New Zealand's West Coast who added much-needed edge and dirtiness to the Wigan side under Mike Gregory, forming a gruesome twosome in the front row with fellow Kiwi Craig Smith. Uncompromising but extremely fit, he boasted the worst suspension record of any NRL player during his time at Sydney Roosters but had the skills to back up his snarl, being rated the world's top prop for a time. A proud Maori, he was a fearsome sight leading his national side's haka and Wigan never really replaced his intimidating presence after the *News of the World* revealed he was suffering from hepatitis B and he was forced to retire.

OTHER SPORTING ACHIEVEMENTS

Athletics Jeff Clare was one of the country's top discus throwers and narrowly missed out on Olympic selection. David Wood was an English Schools finalist in the javelin.

Baseball Jim Sullivan was a Welsh international.

Bowls Derek Brindle and Bill Jolley were both top-class Crown Green exponents and David Stephenson was more than useful.

Boxing Brian McTigue and Jerry Shea were both professionals. Frank Stephens had a fine record as an amateur heavyweight and Bill Sayer, Percy Moxey and William Curran were also highly proficient amateurs. Maurice Lindsay was a formidable 8st boxer in his teens.

Cricket Liam Botham played three first class matches for Hampshire. John Gray was on the books of Warwickshire and the MCC. Martin Offiah played for Essex 2nd XI and appeared in *Wisden*.

Cycling David Booysen was Western Province cycling champion three years in a row.

Darts Shaun Edwards once listed his greatest sporting achievement outside Rugby League as reaching the final of the Scholes Labour Club Darts Competition.

Football John Barton was a 'Busby Babe' at Manchester United but other Wigan players who have been on the books of – or trialled by – top soccer clubs include Denis Betts (Manchester United), Alf Ellaby (Rotherham), Mike Ford (Oldham Athletic), Roy Heaney (Bolton Wanderers), George Johnson (Burnley), Ian Potter (trials with Blackburn Rovers and Liverpool), Johnny Ring (Swansea), Mick Scott (Hull City), Jim Sharrock (Blackburn Rovers) and Stuart Wright (Chester City).

Golf Andy Collier came third in the Dunhill Amateur
  Masters at Woburn in 1987. Jim Sullivan was a 4
  handicapper and almost took up the game professionally.
Ju-Jitsu Kiwi Lance Todd was highly skilled in this martial art.
Water Polo Fred Griffiths was a notable player back in South
  Africa. John Gray represented Coventry.
Wrestling Francis Gregory was amateur heavyweight
  wrestling champion of Cornwall, while Bill Bretherton
  was an ex-professional wrestler.

THE LONG AND THE SHORT OF IT

Wigan's tallest ever first-team players are Wayne McDonald
(2005) and Barrie-Jon Mather (1991–5) who both stand 6ft
7in tall, with the bulkier McDonald probably just shading the
title by a centimetre or so if we go all metric. The identity of
Wigan's shortest first-teamer is harder to definitively pinpoint,
but a prime contender would certainly be South African scrum-
half Tommy Gentles who was signed for no apparent reason
from Rugby Union in 1958. With the name – and indeed the
appearance – of a music hall comedian, Gentles measured 5ft
3in, weighed barely 10st and wore size 4 rugby boots. He had
a big reputation in the 15-a-side code and the club shelled-out
some serious terms to bring him over, but from the moment the
crestfallen Wigan directors watched the diminutive, bespectacled
figure disembarking his aircraft on arrival, it was clear that
breaking into a squad with five already established scrum-halves
wasn't going to be easy. Gentles played 7 games in 14 months
before Wigan ended up doing what they have done several times
over the years and off-loaded someone they didn't want to Leeds.

DID YOU KNOW?

Second-row forward Rob Louw (1985–6) has had a traumatic existence since leaving Wigan. The rugged former Springbok – whose daughter Roxy is one of South Africa's most famous models – has cheated death three times. In 1991 he had to be pulled from the sea after a near-fatal power boat accident during a race. In 2005 he walked away from a plane crash in the Kruger National Park after the Cessna he was a passenger in overshot the runway and landed in trees, missing certain death by inches. In 2009 he was given just three months to live after being diagnosed with an aggressive form of skin cancer only to manage to beat the disease he now campaigns vigorously to combat.

Fans' favourite Va'aiga Tuigamala (1993–7) has opened a funeral director's (Tuigamala & Sons) in New Zealand specialising in Pacific Island funerals. 'Inga' masterminded the extensive ceremony for the late King Taufa'ahau Tupou IV of Tonga in 2006.

Australian international Ian Roberts (1986–7) has taken up acting since his retirement from Rugby League. The 6ft 5in prop appeared in the 2006 film *Superman Returns*, as Riley one of the henchmen employed by Lex Luthor (Kevin Spacey), and was runner-up in the Australian version of *Strictly Come Dancing*.

All-time great scrum-half Andy Gregory was savaged by a Rottweiler in Ince in September 2006 and only escaped the 12st dog's clutches by punching it repeatedly in the face until it let go.

Since ending his playing career, Martin Offiah is combining being an agent, DJ and occasional TV summariser with an apparent attempt to overhaul John Barrowman and Myleene Klass for most career TV appearances. A contestant on the first series of *Strictly Come Dancing*, his myriad other cameos include making it to the final of *Let's Dance for Comic Relief* with a Bollywood routine, an impersonation of Tunde 'Lighthouse Family' Baiyewu on *Stars In Their Eyes* and narrowly losing out to Ruth Madoc of *Hi-de-Hi!* in the series four live final of *I'm Famous and Frightened*. He is also thought to be the only person to have appeared as himself in both *Emmerdale* and *Hollyoaks*. However, his scheduled appearance on *This is Your Life* in 1993 had to be cancelled as his mother broke the rules by telling him what was afoot and he was subsequently forced to look on as Michael Aspel tip-toed on to the pitch after a game with Leeds in September of that year to surprise club captain Dean Bell with the big red book.

Prop Barrie McDermott was the first person in Britain to be restrained by police using CS gas. The 17st hard man apparently became aggressive outside an Oldham nightclub in 1996 forcing worried policemen to use the newly introduced arrest aid.

MATCH SAVERS: FAMOUS TACKLES

John Sherrington on Joe Lyman (Dewsbury), 1929 Challenge
    Cup final
Martin Ryan on Frank Foster (Bradford), 1948 Challenge
    Cup final

Norman Cherrington on Ike Southward (Workington),
    1958 Challenge Cup final
Kris Radlinski on Keiron Cunningham and Tim Jonkers
    (St Helens), 2002 Challenge Cup final
Mick Scott on Garry Clark (Hull KR), 1985 Challenge Cup
    semi-final
Brian Carney on Anthony Sullivan (St Helens), 2001 league

LIKE FATHER, LIKE SON

Some fathers and sons who have both played for Wigan (eldest
first):

Colin and Phil Clarke
Bernard Coyle Sr and Bernard Coyle Jr
Bernard Coyle Jr and Thomas and James Coyle
Keith Holden Sr and Keith Holden Jr
Keiron O'Loughlin and Sean O'Loughlin
Charlie Seeling Sr and Charlie Seeling Jr
Colin Tyrer and Sean Tyrer
Graeme and Dwayne West

IF YOU WANT TO PLAY FOR WIGAN
No. 2: PLAY FOR PATS

Wigan St Patrick's ARLFC is arguably the amateur game's
greatest nursery providing an incredible conveyor belt of
talent for Wigan and a very useful remainder bin for every

other club to check out. Here is a – by no means exhaustive – list of Wigan first-teamers who first caught the eye miring themselves in that uniquely silty Clarington Park mud:

Rob Ball, Bob Beswick, Les Bolton, Jimmy Boylan, Ronnie Braithwaite, Steve Breheny, Shaun Briscoe, Ged Byrne, James Case, Jeff Clare, Phil Clarke, John Clinton, Bernard Coyle Jr, James Coyle, Thomas Coyle, Geoff Cunliffe, Mick Dean, Martin Dermott, Shaun Edwards, Joe Egan, Mike Forshaw, Martin Gleeson, Sean Gleeson, Darrell Goulding, Jimmy Green, Andy Gregory, Tracey Grundy, Frank Halliwell, Teddy Hanley, Bryn Hargreaves, Liam Farrell, Jim Hickey, Keith Holden Jr, Andy Johnson, Jimmy Lowe, Ian Lucas, Joe Lydon, David Marshall, John Mayo, Jim McCormack, Augustine O'Donnell, Keiron O'Loughlin, Sean O'Loughlin, Tony O'Neill, John O'Shea, Gary Owen, Andy Platt, Kris Radlinski, Craig Rodgers, Richard Russell, Ged Stazicker, Trevor Stockley, Ted Toohey, Joel Tomkins, Sam Tomkins, Chris Tuson, Shaun Wane, Jon Whittle, Stephen Wild, David Wood.

PLAYER OF THE DECADE: THE 1950s

Billy Boston (1953–68)

When commercial time travel is finally realised, close relatives and bodily organs will doubtless be sold for the chance to join the unruly queues snaking through Wigan to go and watch 'Billy B' bestride Central Park in his prime. It is the modern Wigan fan's tragedy that for all the phenomenal talent paraded before them in the last 40 years and for all those incredible memories, we are left with the slightly hollow feeling of the truly spoilt, that actually we might still have been denied seeing the greatest of the lot.

The club's record try-scorer and second only to Brian Bevan in the history of the sport, Cardiff-born Billy was a 12½st teenage thoroughbred at the beginning of his career and a no less effective, only slightly slower 15st powerhouse by the end. He rose to prominence playing Army Rugby Union during his National Service, apparently registering 126 tries in one season with the Royal Signals. After he scored 6 in the Army Cup final, Wigan made their move, helping to assuage his father's doubts by spreading £1,500 in used fivers on the family's kitchen table with the promise of the same amount to follow, plus £1,000 expenses.

When Boston arrived in Wigan, 8,500 fans turned up just to see his debut in the 'A' team and after graduating to the firsts, he played just 6 games before being selected for the 1954 Great Britain tour to Australia where he accumulated 36 tries in 18 games. Boston appeared in six Wembley finals and though he was three-times a winner and scored twice in the 1959 final, he always felt regret that he never really 'exploded' in a Challenge Cup final, but there were plenty of other occasions when he did. There were two fine tries in the 1960 Championship Final victory and his personal favourites – a brace of long-distance scores against Leeds in a 1957 Challenge Cup tie to name but two. Like Hanley, Offiah and Robinson only more so, the crowd came alive every time the ball went his way and he seldom disappointed, allying tremendous running ability to a fearsome hand-off and big-hitting tackling.

He was immensely popular at Central Park and throughout the game, but like most of Wigan's great players his career wasn't all plain sailing. In 1956, he was suspended for 'events before, during and after' a 10–11 Challenge Cup semi-final defeat to Halifax. Boston had told the board he was unfit to play due to an ankle injury but was persuaded and scored a typically unstoppable try, carrying two tacklers over with him, an action that worsened his ankle. Later, centre Jack Broome was injured, Boston was moved inside and his opposite number scored twice. He was blamed, and taking it hard, announced he would give up and return to Cardiff. Eventually he made his peace but confessed to feeling the pressure of his reputation and losing confidence. Coach Joe Egan played a huge part in rescuing a legendary career that had only just begun and despite being transfer-listed briefly in 1963 over more disagreement over an injury, Boston stayed with a club and a town where he was almost a deity, later running the Griffin; a pub less than one of his interception try's length away from Central Park and a match-day shrine for fans of all ages and affiliations to come and pay homage to a true one-off.

Appearances: 488 • Tries: 478 • Goals: 7 • Points: 1,488 • Honours: League Championship 1960; Challenge Cup 1958, 1959, 1965; Lancashire Cup 1966; Lancashire League Championship 1959, 1962

THE ONES THAT GOT AWAY

In October 1994, an agent approached Wigan with the news that a little-known teenage All Black might be interested in a return to the 13-a-side code he first played as a youngster at Auckland's Manukau club. With Jason Robinson and Martin Offiah already on their books, the board weren't interested. A little over a year later, they found themselves pondering a move of £2 million to sign the same man after his efforts in the 1995 Rugby Union World Cup. His name, of course, was Jonah Lomu.

In the summer of 1957, Wigan and St Helens were both chasing a man they termed a 'film star capture': South African speedster Tom van Vollenhoven. Both clubs faced immense difficulties co-ordinating their pursuits from north-west England. In readiness, Wigan chairman Bill Gore had his smallpox and yellow fever vaccinations and planned an extraordinary odyssey to the Cape. His itinerary was to be as follows: train to London, flight to Zurich, from there to Copenhagen, then direct to Nairobi, Kenya. He would then travel overland to Salisbury (now Harare, Zimbabwe), the nearest major city to van Vollenhoven's workplace at the Chingola copper mines located still 600 miles away in what is now Zambia. Van Vollenhoven understandably auctioned his services to the highest bidder before Gore needed to leave and legend has it that had a telegram delivery boy not had to stop to mend his puncture by the side of the road, Wigan might have beaten their old rivals to the signature and enjoyed the mouth-watering prospect of 'Van the Man' lining up on the opposite wing to Billy Boston for the next decade.

In October 1992, former Olympic 200m finalist Ade Mafe contacted Wigan with a view to undergoing a trial period in the 'A' team at Central Park. As someone capable of running 20.5 seconds for the 200m at his peak, he would have given even Martin Offiah a scare in tick and pass but though Mafe did indeed come to Wigan, a switch to League proved too difficult and probably too late. Similarly, in 1963, Wigan were reported to have signed Scottish sprint champion Ricky

Dunbar, a winner of Edinburgh's world-famous Powderhall Sprint and a world professional 120yds record holder. 'The Flying Scotsman' could well have gone on to become the fastest Wigan winger of all time, but chose instead to move to Australia and run professionally.

Singer and Radio 2 presenter Sir Jimmy Young was a nippy wing three-quarter in his youth playing Rugby Union in Gloucestershire. During wartime military training at Compton Bassett in Wiltshire, he befriended Jack Hesketh, whose father was a Wigan director. The two men trained at Central Park on their weekend leaves but Sir Jimmy declined the opportunity of a trial. He went on to have five top ten hits in the UK (including two number ones) and a hugely successful afternoon radio show.

In August 1983, Wigan announced the signings of Kiwi duo Shane Varley and Howie Tamati on 1-year deals with the option of an extension to 3 years should it suit both parties. Varley jetted in on 8 September only to be met by officials from Leigh who claimed they had an agreement with the New Zealand Rugby League and spirited him away to Hilton Park where he signed. Tamati joined Wigan as planned and enjoyed a Wembley visit in his only season. Had Varley taken up his potential 3 years in the Cherry and White, he would have enjoyed two Wembley visits in addition to collecting Lancashire Cup and John Player Trophy winners' medals but I'm sure he never even thinks about that now.

HIDEOUS INJURIES

Zimbabwe-born wing Trevor Lake was clearly tougher than his lithe frame suggested, as in his younger days he survived a collision with a speeding giraffe.

Jack Hilton received serious wounds to his right thigh from a German shell in North Africa during the Second World War but came back to score 122 tries in 137 appearances for Wigan.

During a 16–6 league defeat at Widnes on 29 January 1986, Australian prop Greg Dowling was temporarily blinded by lime markings on the pitch.

Enjoying a pre-season warm weather training trip to Portugal in 2004, Kevin Brown sustained serious cuts when he ran through a glass patio door he thought was open. He severed an artery in his bicep and had to be immediately flown home for surgery.

In the 1988/89 season, Martin Dermott was told to stay away from training after developing a mysterious rash. It turned out he was allergic to his new bedding.

During a spell working as a golf greenkeeper in his first season, Andy Goodway accidentally put a pitchfork through his foot.

Billy Boston almost missed the 1961 Challenge Cup final after falling awkwardly when running in a dummy try on an empty Wembley pitch for the benefit of BBC TV cameras. In the end, Wigan gave him several painkilling injections and selected him because of the psychological edge he gave.

Steve Hampson missed three consecutive Challenge Cup finals because of three separate injuries. He broke his leg in 1984, his wrist in 1985 and his arm in 1988. Luckily for 'Hampo' he played for Wigan in an era of unprecedented success so, his jinx eventually wore off and he was still able to collect five winners' medals and score two cup final tries.

Shaun Edwards missed four games in December 1988 due to contracting chicken pox.

In the 1963 Challenge Cup final, David Bolton was knocked cold and taken from the field for almost 20 minutes, during which time two St John Ambulance men somewhat hastily announced to his wife, Betty, that Dave was dead. He eventually returned to the game and woozily aimed a pass in Eric Ashton's direction that was intercepted by Lance Todd Trophy-winner Harold Poynton for a crucial score. Wakefield won 25–10.

In 1985, prop Neil Courtney landed awkwardly when training alone with a tackle bag. He dislocated his shoulder so badly the bone severed an artery and cut through nerve tissue. He nearly lost his life and, after being rushed to Wigan Infirmary, was left with a partially paralysed left arm.

Australian three-quarter Jamie Ainscough was forced to retire after a freak arm injury. In July 2002, he caught Saints centre Martin Gleeson across the mouth in a tackle and part of Gleeson's tooth broke off and embedded itself in Ainscough's arm, neither player noticed and the fragment wasn't discovered until Ainscough complained of lingering pain many weeks later. The arm had developed a bone infection and surgery had to be performed with a risk of necessary amputation. In the end, he was given the all-clear but still needs regular checks to ensure infection has not recurred.

In 1993, just months before he joined Wigan, Va'aiga Tuigamala was punched in the back of the head playing Rugby Union against Tonga in Nuku'alofa. He was knocked unconscious, stopped breathing and was effectively paralysed from the waist down. Fortunately, prompt medical attention ensured he was soon able to make a full recovery.

During a game against Hull at the Boulevard in 1990, Kiwi tough-guy Dean Bell clashed heads with Denis Betts, knocking Betts out cold. Bell reached to stem the blood flow from his mouth only to be unable to actually find his bottom lip because it had split into two distinct, jagged parts severing two arteries. Bell could easily have lost his lip without the prompt treatment of the Wigan club doctor, Ansar Zaman, who put in 33 stitches which had to be restitched without anaesthetic a few days later after splitting apart when Bell bit into a chicken sandwich. The doctor said Bell's pain would be acute, like having a mouth full of razor blades but he actually had to be dissuaded from playing in Wigan's next match against Australia! Bell also probably had his life saved by Wigan's physio after he was knocked unconscious and swallowed his tongue in the 1993 Challenge Cup semi-final at Elland Road.

TOP O' T' POPS

Wigan players who have released singles:

'Sin in the City' – Massey (a band made up of Henry Paul, his brother Robbie and a friend. The song was apparently a mixture of rap and soul)

'Touch Down (For Your Love)' – Martin Offiah (inevitably, it was a sort of dance track)

'The Song Will Always Be the Same' – Henderson Gill (a rap record that apparently 'sounds like he played: tough and uncompromising')

'Am I Ever Going to See the Biff Again?' – Matthew Johns (In the guise of his TV alter ego Reg Regan. It actually got into the Australian top 20 – mind you, how hard can that be?)

'The Wigan Rugby Song' – John 'Mr Riverside' Martin and the squad's Christmas 1986 masterpiece may have sounded like a collaboration between Black Lace, the Houghton Weavers and a colliery choir, but any fan of a certain age can probably still summon the lyrics without much trouble ('. . . marching off to Wemberlee and singing with the band, etc.')

TEN GREAT: WEMBLEY TRIES

1 Martin Offiah v Leeds, 1994

The game's greatest showman finally fulfilled his destiny in the game's greatest showpiece. Having four times failed to get to Wembley with Widnes, Offiah collected the Lance Todd on his first visit with Wigan in 1992 but was still left feeling somewhat bereft after officialdom dubiously ruled out the historic hat-trick-sealing score he had promised. The following year, his main contribution was in providing a head for red-carded Richie Eyres to apply his elbow to, so in 1994 – 13 minutes into a scorching afternoon – he gratefully seized his chance to move alongside Geoff Hurst, Freddie Mercury and a white horse as a genuine Wembley icon. Taking up the ball just a couple of metres from his own line, 'Chariots' sliced past two forwards and accelerated clear of Francis Cummins before sweeping past Alan Tait on the outside. He scored several tries to rank with this during his Wigan career, but sinking to his knees, head in hands at the end of his poetic sprint, his body language spoke less of ecstasy and more of relief in knowing that he had at last delivered an enduring masterpiece on the biggest stage in a way very few of the best ever really do.

2 Trevor Lake v Hunslet, 1965

Lake's spectacular flying touchdown through John Griffiths' challenge is one of the iconic images in Wigan history. In what was already a classic match, full-back Ray Ashby began the move with a Lance Todd-guaranteeing 30yd burst, before Lake appeared in support at halfway. The African gazelle held off the chasers over the remaining 50yds ending with a high-risk dive captured by every camera in the stadium. For once, even Eddie Waring's strangled commentary seemed to add to the try's excitement: 'This is Ashby running . . . surely he'll not go the length of the field . . . nobody will catch this feller, nobody will catch him, nobody will catch him!'

3 Ellery Hanley v St Helens, 1989

The stunning try that ensured it wouldn't just be the scoreline Wigan fans could treasure forever. Receiving the ball from

Shaun Edwards just inside the Saints' half there appeared to be nothing much on, only for the superhuman Wigan skipper to slalom his way through five defenders – Bernard Dwyer, Paul Vautin, Phil Veivers, Gary Connolly and Paul Groves – to score with a barely a hand laid on him. It showcased skills, power and determination from another dimension and it broke the already fragile Saints.

4 Henderson Gill v Hull, 1985

There are at least three Wigan tries from 1985 worthy of a place in this list but Gill's is – just – the most memorable, mainly for the chunky wing's joyous celebration. Mike Ford found Brett Kenny, he provided a lovely long pass to David Stephenson and the centre set the power-packed Gill storming past Gary Kemble from 75yds, his eyes intently fixed on the distant try-line before he supplied a huge, gum shield-revealing celebratory smile, an image almost as historic as Trevor Lake's dive 20 years before.

5 Stan Jolley v Wakefield, 1946

Anxious to make amends for a badly missed tackle in the first half which allowed Wakefield to take a 6–3 lead, Jolley seized on a loose ball and raced 70yds through the Trinity defence for one of the finest solo tries in a Challenge Cup final.

6 Ellery Hanley v Halifax, 1988

From a restart, full-back Joe Lydon scorched 70yds in the manner of his 1984 display for Widnes against Wigan. He found Hanley on his inside and the loose forward deftly evaded Halifax chasers with a remarkable crab-like run across field to score under the posts.

7 Syd Abram v Dewsbury, 1929

Rugby League's first Wembley try would surely merit inclusion even if it wasn't a classic, but luckily it was. After Len Mason, Johnny Ring and Frank Stephens combined to put Hindley lad Abram in space, the stand-off used wing Lou Brown as a foil to sprint 40yds to the corner.

8 Mark Preston v Warrington, 1990

Preston had already scored one 80yd interception try in the first half but was on hand to round off this magnificent length-of-the-field team move in the second. Adrian Shelford won the ball and found Andy Goodway, who released Steve Hampson into a gap. Hampson found Hanley who carried the ball deep into the opposition half before handing on to the seriously injured Shaun Edwards, though he was prevented from scoring by one of the great cover tackles from Mike Gregory. Gregory had tracked the move all the way only to look up and see Preston accept a pass out of contact to scramble over in the corner.

9 Mick Sullivan v Hull, 1959

As Hull lost the ball close to the Wigan line, stand-off Dave Bolton collected, beat two defenders, sent out a wide pass to Sullivan and Wigan's record signing hurtled 75 yards down the left wing to stretch Wigan's lead.

10 Jason Robinson v Leeds, 1995

Still smarting from being left out of the previous year's final against his home-town club, 'Billy Whizz' was fired up for the rematch and scored two sizzling tries. His second was marginally the better as he took advantage of some slack marking at the play the ball to career through a group of six shell-shocked defenders.

CHANGING ROOMS (FEATURING BAD LANGUAGE, NUDITY & VIOLENCE)

On 20 February 1983, Granada TV decided to show highlights of Wigan against Hull KR at Central Park on their new *Rugby League Action* programme. Wigan lost 21–5 and cameras followed the beaten side into the dingy, steamy confines of the home dressing room just in time to witness a furious, scattergun tirade of swearing and abuse from the coach Alex Murphy. Facing weeks of criticism for his outmoded man-management style – it wasn't just the swear words, but also the way he picked on David Stephenson – Murphy claimed he had been told the cameras were just there to film some motivational posters and that during his rant they were actually turned off.

On Saturday 3 February 1990, Granada's intrepid cameras provided live coverage of Wigan's crucial league fixture at Widnes. It proved to be a TV classic: a calmly taken penalty by 18-year-old Bobby Goulding in the dying seconds secured the visitors a dramatic 11–10 victory and a 2-point lead at the top of the Stones Bitter Championship. After the obligatory commercial break, Granada decided to cut to their camera in the away dressing room to see 'just what that victory meant to Wigan' and as well as one or two suitably pleased-looking players, viewers at home were treated to a full-frontal nude shot of the oblivious Goulding as he removed his towel fresh out of the shower. In the days before live broadcasting's 10-second obscenity delay, the director was forced to hurriedly cut back to Rob McCaffrey and Brian Smith on the gantry.

On 10 March 1974, Wigan played Warrington at Central Park in the Challenge Cup third round. As usual, the game was notable for an enormous amount of needle. Colin Clarke had seen red for a high tackle in the first half and in the second half, Wigan loose forward Eddie Cunningham and Warrington hard man Mike Nicholas were dismissed for fighting. Nicholas was incensed, even throwing a punch at team-mate Alan Whittle who tried to calm him down. After both men disappeared down the tunnel, Warrington sent their trainer to talk to Nicholas, but he couldn't be found in the away dressing room. Suddenly, the trainer heard screams coming from the home changing room and burst in to find Nicholas attempting to strangle Cunningham in the bath.

At the Central Park homecoming following Wigan's 1994 Wembley victory, travelling reserves Neil Cowie and Jason Robinson decided to take out their frustrations with some apparently traditional light vandalism in the home changing rooms. As Robinson flailed about with a lump hammer, Cowie charged across the room and butted the false wall dividing the room from the corridor, his head went straight through the plasterboard and his ears got stuck, lodging him in position staring out at the corridor like a trophy stag's head above the fireplace of a country pub.

PLAYER OF THE DECADE: THE 1960s

Eric Ashton MBE (1955–69)
Few will now recall Bert Marsh, the pub crooner in Standishgate's Royal Oak in the 1950s, but his name deserves

to go down in Wigan history for a reason other than his voice: Bert alerted the club (via the landlord and Wigan director Billy Wood) to Eric Ashton. Marsh had been stationed with the Argyll and Sutherland Highlanders in Edinburgh and had encountered a 6ft 2in St Helenser carving out a reputation as a Services Rugby Union player and sprinter. Ashton had trialled unsuccessfully with Saints before his National Service but Wigan directors nonetheless travelled up to see him and secured his verbal agreement to come and trial at the end of his military service. His eventual 6-match trial lasted just one game before he was offered £150 to sign.

Tall, elegant and clean-cut, Ashton was to go on to become the Bobby Moore of Rugby League and it is hard to think of any player held in such affection by both Wigan and St Helens. He made his debut as a winger outside Ernie Ashcroft in a 52–5 victory over Dewsbury at Central Park in 1955 scoring two tries while a man named Boston grabbed seven on the other wing! The two were to go on to form possibly the greatest centre/wing pairing in Rugby League history, playing 246 times together down the right wing; their beautifully executed scissors move snipped defences to ribbons for years. Ashton was a creative centre who played to his winger and, when Boston was that winger the result was usually a try for the great man or a dummy and try for Ashton.

Appointed team captain just 2 years into his Wigan career, he remained skipper for the rest of his time at Central Park, leading the club in a record six Wembley finals. Eric also captained Great Britain on tour in 1962 as they comfortably won the Ashes. In 1960, he became disillusioned with Wigan, primarily because of disagreement over injury compensation but also because of persistent heckling from some fans dissatisfied with his form. He was listed at a record fee of

£13,000 and despite bids from St Helens and Workington, he made up with the board and came off.

Appointed player-coach in 1963, he fulfilled the role for a decade before leaving to become coach at Leeds and, after tiring of the travelling, then at St Helens, the club who had turned him down 20 years earlier.

**Appearances: 497 • Tries: 231 • Goals: 448 •
Points: 1,589 • Honours: League Championship 1960;
Challenge Cup 1958, 1959, 1965; Lancashire Cup 1966;
Lancashire League Championship 1959, 1962;
BBC2 Floodlit Trophy 1968**

IT'S AN HONOUR

In June 1966, Wigan's Eric Ashton became the first Rugby League player to receive an honour when he was awarded the MBE. Since then, nine more Wigan players have been 'gonged':

Chris Hesketh MBE January 1976
Cec Mountford MBE January 1987
Ellery Hanley MBE January 1990
Shaun Edwards OBE January 1996
Billy Boston MBE June 1996
Martin Offiah MBE January 1997
Jason Robinson MBE January 2004 and OBE January 2008
Andy Farrell OBE January 2005
Kris Radlinski MBE June 2007

UNCLE JOE'S TO UNCLE SAM

On 10 June 1989, Wigan journeyed to America to take on Warrington in an exhibition match at the County Stadium in Milwaukee, sometime home of the Green Bay Packers American Football team. Wigan won 12–5, with an Andy Goodway try and 4 Joe Lydon goals bettering 2 John Woods penalties and a drop goal. 7,773 turned up to watch.

WIGAN ON STRIKE

In February 1920, Wigan's forwards decided to take a stand at being paid less than their colleagues in the backs by refusing to travel to Swinton for the upcoming league fixture. The backs came out in solidarity and despite the club rounding up willing local amateurs to meet at the station and travel to fulfil the fixture, the game didn't happen, although no one thought to tell Runcorn-based forward Ernie Shaw who had gone straight to Station Road and found himself doing a very lonely warm-up on the pitch. The dispute eventually went to arbitration with Percy Coldrick and Charlie Seeling arguing for the pack men against the Wigan board. The result was that they failed to make a satisfactory case for a pay rise but that the question of preferential pay for backs should be revised by the committee before next season.

If the 1920s was a time of widespread industrial action, so too were the 1970s and in November 1977, Wigan were on strike again after a row over bonus payments escalated following a JPS Trophy win over New Hunslet. The match bonus was £55, a tenner over basic pay, but the players wanted an extra £35. The board maintained bonuses took into account opponents' form, standing and the size of the gate, and refused to be threatened or dictated to. As a result, a collection of 'A' teamers and trialists took on Warrington in the next league fixture and lost 24-9. 'A' team coach Peter Smethurst played as captain and brought all the players a chicken as a bonus (he was a butcher), an anonymous fan donated a jubilee crown to each player and the match sponsors gave each of them a tankard and share of the man of the match prize money. After a similar line-up went out of the JPS Trophy 25–0 at Widnes, coach Vince Karalius stepped in to act as mediator and the dispute was settled just in time to take on New Hunslet again in the league. There was no bonus row this time as Wigan lost 9–7!

DID YOU KNOW?

The two highest points-scorers in international Rugby Union history, Jonny Wilkinson (England) and Neil Jenkins (Wales), were both keen Wigan fans as youngsters and visited Central Park on a number of occasions. World Cup-winner Will Greenwood is a big Wigan fan and England coach and legendary skipper Martin Johnson was brought up being forced to watch Rugby League on the telly by his Wiganer father.

Eight Wigan players have featured in a Rugby Union World Cup playing squad. Chris Ashton may well be the ninth in 2011. The list comprises:

Frano Botica (New Zealand) 1987, Brian Carney (Ireland) 2007, Andy Craig (Scotland) 2003, Andy Farrell (England) 2007, Scott Quinnell (Wales) 1999, Jason Robinson (England) 2003 and 2007, Shem Tatupu (Western Samoa) 1995, Va'aiga Tuigamala (New Zealand) 1991.

Giant South African star Nick du Toit is unique in that he won a Challenge Cup winners' medal before ever playing in the competition. The all-action centre or second row was on the bench for Wigan's 1985 triumph over Hull but couldn't be risked in the unbearably tense closing stages, meaning he didn't actually get a game until the first-round tie with Workington in 1986. Incidentally, Nick is also the only professional Rugby League player to have won the top prize on Paul Daniels' BBC quiz *Every Second Counts*.

Wigan's sensational World Club Challenge trip to Brisbane in 1994 was notable for another world-class sporting achievement. According to the August 1994 edition of *Wisden Cricket Monthly*: 'Wigan and Great Britain Rugby League prop forward Neil Cowie drank fifty-one cans of lager on the flight from Australia to England, breaking the record set by Australian batsman David Boon in 1989.'

During the 1988 Ashes series, Andy Gregory gave an interview to Sydney's 2UE radio station and used the phrase 'you know' 108 times in just over 3 minutes. The clip became an often-played favourite that year.

ENTRANCE MUSIC

Some tunes Wigan have come out to over the years:
'Entry of the Gladiators' – Julius Fucik
'O Fortuna' – Carl Orff
'Conquest of Paradise' – Vangelis
'Now We Are Free' – Dreamgate

TEN GREAT: GOAL KICKERS

In no particular order, a selection of some of the finest boots to wear the Cherry and White:

1 Jim Sullivan (2,317 goals) The Welshman's goal tally speaks for itself: he just didn't miss. Sullivan could manage great distances (he landed a 65yd penalty on his debut for Great Britain against Australia in 1924), tight angles, and in the days of lengthy kicking duels between opposing full-backs, had a great tactical brain.

2 Frano Botica (840 goals) Having struggled to get into the All Blacks Rugby Union team because of Grant Fox's supposed superiority as a goalkicker, Botica practiced his kicking religiously in a bid to cement a place in Wigan's star-studded team. His accuracy was so unerring that Wigan fans mentally counted in 6s whenever tries were scored. Proficient from either touchline and from anywhere in the opposition half, his kicks always seemed to have just the requisite strength to glide gently over the bar, no matter how near or far they were taken from. Frano was the fastest man to 1,000 points in Rugby League history (93 matches) and broke Wigan's record for goals in a season for the second time with a total of 186 in 1994/95.

3 Andy Farrell (1,335 goals) He seemed able to do everything else, so it was no surprise when 'Faz' turned out to be a brilliant natural goal-kicker. As possibly the biggest man to have regularly kicked goals for Wigan, he clearly had power and distance on his side but was also remarkably proficient from anywhere. Predominantly left-footed, his biggest attribute was surely his mental strength in that he never seemed to miss the really important kicks, often nervelessly nailing late, match-deciding conversions.

4 Colin Tyrer (813 goals) Tyrer took an awfully long time over his goal kicks, to the extent that 'doing a Tyrer' was for many years the industry expression for overly methodical place-kickers, but his method worked and he became such a weapon that when Castleford brutally took him out at Wembley in 1970 they basically guaranteed themselves the cup.

5 Fred Griffiths (663 goals) 'Punchy' was a powerful South African full-back who, during his stint, was widely acknowledged as the club's finest kicker since Sullivan. His club record 176 goals in a season stood for 34 years but always looked vulnerable when a kicker of Frano Botica's quality joined Wigan's free-scoring 1990s team.

6 John Gray (130 goals) A skilled, ball-playing hooker or prop signed from English Rugby Union in 1973, Gray also possessed a kicking game as impressive as his moustache and sideburns. His move to Australian side North Sydney saw him revolutionise place-kicking Down Under by placing the ball vertically and kicking from the side, running 'round the corner' to ensure greater surface area contact with the ball. This sacrificed some distance but greatly increased accuracy. In the land of the front-on toe kickers it quickly became the norm and Gray earned himself a reputation as a kicking innovator.

7 Ken Gee (508 goals) An unmistakeable figure with his trademark scrum cap, the stocky Gee was not just scrum ballast in the manner of many forwards of his time, he could run, pass and was a deadly accurate kicker of goals. He didn't kick regularly for Wigan until late in his legendary career but he quickly took to it, finishing his first kicking season (1949/50) as the Rugby League's joint top goal-scorer with 133. Apparently Gee started at the age of 14, taking kicks on the field adjoining his workplace – Pemberton Colliery – whenever he could.

8 Pat Richards (289 goals) The towering Australian with the mighty boot had an indifferent first year in Wigan colours as he was shunted from centre to wing to full-back, dropped, then recalled in a manner that typified the Warriors' crisis-hit 2006 season. The following year saw him improving out of sight after being entrusted with the regular goal-kicking duties. He quickly became Wigan's major source of points and such a reliable kicker that it was rumoured he was interesting American Football teams.

9 George Fairbairn (594 goals) Unlike Botica, Sullivan and others, the hirsute Scot didn't have the luxury of kicking goals in an already strong side. In the dark days of the late

1970s, Fairbairn's boot was frequently Wigan's likeliest source of points, an expectation that brought the sort of pressure he thrived on. He made such a good job of it that he became the regular kicker for the various international sides he represented as well.

10 Joe Lydon (309 goals) Though chiefly remembered for a catalogue of glittering long-range tries for club and country, Lydon's exceptional long-range kicking ability was a deadly weapon that came to Wigan's rescue on a number of occasions. Everyone recalls his fabled 61-yd drop goal (the longest on record) to break Warrington's resistance in the 1989 Challenge Cup semi-final at Maine Road, but there was also a last-minute drop in a snowstorm at Halifax in the 1993 quarter-final and the vital penalty against Bradford in a Central Park mudbath in 1988 that earned a retro-looking 2–0 win and kicked off Wigan's 8-year domination of the competition. By reputation a big-match player, his nonchalant kicking style gave off an air of reluctance but he frequently seemed to find his groove when most necessary.

PLAYER OF THE DECADE: THE 1970s

George Fairbairn (1974–81)

The Bills Francis and Ashurst might have cause to complain about this selection, but in a period of Wigan history that won't be fondly recalled, George Fairbairn stood out. The bearded Scotsman was a powerful runner and rugged defender and, as well as being a very useful goal-kicker, he became the club's player-coach at just 25, leading Wigan back out of the Second

Division and into a Lancashire Cup final before leaving for a record transfer fee. Wigan's only Great Britain tourist in 1979, it is a mark of his ability that he won the Man of Steel award in 1980, performing for a club that was relegated from the top flight.

George only arrived at Wigan by chance: former Wigan star Johnny Lawrenson called on a butcher in Kelso on his way home from a Scottish holiday. The butcher was George 'Happy' Wilson, Lawrenson's former Workington team-mate and when asked by Lawrenson if there were any good players in the area, he immediately replied, 'Yes, George Fairbairn, the Kelso full-back.' Since the legendary Andy Irvine was blocking Fairbairn's path to regular Scottish Union honours, Lawrenson passed the information on to the Wigan board and after a trip to the Borders to check him out, he was soon signed for a reported £8,000 fee. He made his debut on the left wing against Dewsbury in November 1974, scoring a try, but was swiftly switched to full-back and never looked back, going on to win Lancashire and England honours, somewhat bizarrely for a born-and-bred Scotsman.

After being relieved of the coaching position in the wake of Wigan's promotion, he moved to Hull KR for a world record £72,500 fee and began to win the silverware he had always deserved. Week in, week out in the midst of disappointments, rows and strikes, George maintained Wigan's boast of providing world-class players for the fans to watch.

Appearances: 207 • Tries: 30 • Goals: 594 •
Points: 1,267 • Honours: None but lots with Hull KR!

VIPs

The guest of honour at the 1992 Challenge Cup final was the recently re-elected Prime Minister John Major, and after Wigan's victory, he decided to pop into the dressing rooms to congratulate them. As he passed the showers, he encountered eccentric second-row forward Billy McGinty wearing nothing but what he claimed was a pineapple ring as a genital appendage. 'Last time I eat pineapple,' remarked Major, not knowing quite where to look as McGinty strutted past. It transpired that the reality was less fruity, as, according to Billy the 'pineapple' was actually a piece of yellow sponge he used to cover a cut on his knee. Nevertheless, various tabloid newspapers were soon on the phone and even ran features on the hole-widths of various leading pineapple ring brands. The meeting was captured by a camera crew making a documentary about Wigan and has now become so legendary that it can only be a matter of time before it is made into an *Invictus* style film with George Clooney as Major and Andy Serkis as either McGinty or the pineapple ring.

Field Marshal Montgomery was the guest of honour at the 1963 Challenge Cup final and as Eric Ashton introduced him to the Wigan side, team joker Frank Collier told the 75-year-old war hero that he had fought under him at El Alamein. 'Did you?' asked Monty, even though the 29-year-old second row would only have been 8 at the time. 'What regiment?' he enquired. 'The Girl Guides,' Collier replied, smiling. 'The finest regiment ever,' the great man retorted, patting him on the back. Shortly afterwards, on his way up to the Royal Box, the Eighth Army commander asked RFL executive Bill Fallowfield, 'What regiment did that big chap say he was in again?'

In 1932, the then Prince of Wales (later King Edward VIII) visited Central Park as part of a tour of Lancashire's 'distressed areas'. He became the first member of the royal family to see a game of Rugby League as he watched Jim Sullivan referee a match between two teams of unemployed youths and remarked that Central Park '. . . isn't a very good ground is it?' which, for me at least, is a far more shocking pronouncement than his abdication as king in 1936.

THE GREATEST WEMBLEY: 1965 v 1985

8 May 1965, Wigan 20 Hunslet 16
Team: Ashby (LTT), Boston, Ashton (g), Holden (t), Lake (2t), Hill, Parr, Gardiner, Clarke, McTigue, Stephens, Evans, Gilfedder (t, 3g)

Summary: This was a superb, nail-biting Challenge Cup final. Star-studded aristocrats Wigan took on unfancied, shock finalists Hunslet in a feast of relentlessly fast open rugby, the closeness of the fixture reflected by the first joint winners of the Lance Todd Trophy: Wigan full-back Ray Ashby and Hunslet stand-off Brian Gabbitas.

Main Men: Loose forward Laurie Gilfedder gave Wigan the lead with a penalty after just 33 seconds and, 4 minutes after the interval, sprinted 45yds for a glorious score in the corner. Zimbabwean wing Trevor Lake scored two tries including one of the finest ever, Brian McTigue was the usual tower of strength and centre Keith Holden took advantage of the strict policing of the Ashton/Boston wing to score one smart try and lay on another for Lake. Ex-Liverpool City player Ashby, however, was a revelation, constantly linking up from full-back and having a hand in two tries. For an inspired Hunslet, Gabbitas was obviously outstanding and pulled all the attacking strings. Billy Langton kicked well, second rows Geoff Gunney and Bill Ramsey were at the heart of everything, centre Geoff Shelton scored a fabulous first-half try and wing John Griffiths outran four defenders for his 65th-minute score having had one disallowed in the first half.

Turning Points: The botched kick-off was a disappointing rather than terminal start for Hunslet, but the Yorkshiremen would point to John Griffiths' disallowed 13th-minute try, the touch judge claiming Lake pushed him in touch at a time when taking a lead might have been vital. More likely, the game turned when Hunslet blew three consecutive second-half scoring opportunities through poor passing and just after the third, the man having the game of his life, Ray Ashby, broke from deep to put Lake zooming away and Wigan 20–9 up with 20 minutes to go.

4 May 1985, Wigan 28 Hull 24

Team: Edwards (t), Ferguson (2t), Stephenson (g), Donlan, Gill (t, 3g), Kenny (t, LTT), Ford, Courtney, Kiss, Case, West, Dunn, Potter. Subs: Campbell, du Toit

Summary: It would be a contrary Wigan fan who wouldn't argue pretty strongly for this being quite simply the finest game of anything ever. This match set the big occasion bar impossibly high, even for the lucky Wigan fans of the next fifteen years. Few can have subsequently taken their seats before a major RL final without thinking 'Am I about to see a "1985" again?' Both sides produced coruscating highs for their fans, but for Wiganers the tries were of a calibre undreamed of when watching dire Second Division rugby just 4 years earlier. Betamax videos were worn out as the game became almost a set text for supporters; indeed for those of a certain age. Ray French and Alex Murphy's words of wisdom can still be called up from failing memory banks with all the alacrity of a Victorian child conjugating Latin verb forms. Even the BBC realised they had inadvertently broadcast something special, repeating it several times that year, including a showing at Christmas.

Main Men: A record 10 overseas players were involved and while they provided much of the stardust, there were some impressive British displays too: 19-year-old Mike Ford won a 14in colour TV as the non-overseas player of the match (who needs the Lance Todd?), Henderson Gill and Shaun Edwards defended well and scored tries to remember, Gill also kicked three vital goals but it was the Aussie duo of Ferguson and Kenny who won Wigan the game. Ferguson flew over from Australia and in between cigarettes, collected two great tries – the first all footwork from a standing start in what to a normal human would have been tight space, the second an opportunist 50m breakaway. Kenny was something else again: he ambled out for the kick-off, hands in pockets with all the moustachioed indifference of a moody Western gunslinger and proceeded to have a hand in 4 of his team's 5 tries with his long passes and sharp breaks; he even scored a fabulous one of his own with an extra-terrestrial burst of speed over 50yds to take him outside Gary Kemble at full-back. For Hull, Kenny's Parramatta half-back partner Peter Sterling produced an all-time great display that would have won him the Lance Todd and a winner's medal in any other year, James Leuluai – who just six weeks after this game became father to current Wigan star Tommy – produced two quality finishes to set up the grandstand finish and veteran loose forward, Hull legend Steve 'Knocker' Norton was behind much of Hull's fightback.

Turning Points: 21-year-old Hull prop Lee Crooks only managed one kick at goal and this was ultimately crucial in a game of 5 tries each. The introduction of Hull youngsters Gary Divorty and Garry Schofield with 22 minutes remaining turned the game on its head to such an extent – the 'Airlie Birds' running in three unanswered tries – that Hull's shades-sporting, cigar-smoking coach Arthur Bunting must have rued not starting with the pair. However, with hindsight, the key moment was probably John Muggleton and Dane O'Hara's 51st-minute failure to collect a pass which enabled Ferguson to hare away for Wigan's final try and provide – just – the necessary amount of daylight.

TALKING TURKEY

Team captain Doug Laughton's departure from Wigan in 1973 was partly due to controversy over a roast turkey. Tiring of the regulation mixed grill the players were fed on their way back from Yorkshire away fixtures, the combative loose forward swapped his meal for the club chairman's far more appetising roast turkey. He was halfway through it before the 'mix up' was discovered by the furious chairman who shouted, 'Right, Laughton! You're going on the transfer list tomorrow.' And indeed he did, moving to Widnes for £6,000 very shortly after.

Meanwhile, in other turkey news, Andy Goodway, Wigan's £65,000 signing from Oldham in 1985, enjoyed a 'bad boy' reputation at Watersheddings and part of the reason for this and Oldham's willingness to let him go was because he was rumoured to have taken the turkey earmarked from the club's Christmas meat raffle.

TWICKERS IN A TWIST

Barrie-Jon Mather was the first Wigan Rugby League player to go on to play for England in the Five Nations, but centre David Stephenson could have beaten him by 16 years: he was actually called up as a reserve by England for their Five Nations match with France at Twickenham on 15 January 1983. A former Fylde RU player, Stephenson had been playing League for more than 4 years at this point and, tempted though he was to report for duty and see what happened, he got in contact to say he would be unavailable due to training for Wigan's Rugby League game against Workington at Derwent Park the very next day. Air Commodore (naturally) Bob Weighill, who had signed the invite, said notification had been sent to one of the wrong two Stephensons on the RFU contacts list.

PLAYER OF THE DECADE: THE 1980s

Shaun Edwards OBE (1983–97)

There were legends everywhere in Wigan's 1980s teams and though it seems wrong to choose anyone other than Hanley to represent this period, it is the measure of one man that actually his selection will brook little argument and that man is, of course, Shaun Edwards.

Signed rather theatrically at midnight on his 17th birthday for a record fee for an amateur (£35,000) in a ceremony shown on the new-fangled breakfast TV, Edwards had already captained England Schoolboys at League and Union and with a father who had played for Warrington before injury ended his career, he had not just been steeped but methodically

schooled in Rugby League from an early age. Young Shaun
had pace, all the skills and was showing signs of the sort of
intense, single-minded, winning-is-everything mentality that
few players truly possess now and certainly didn't then. After
years of letting their best talent go to other clubs, his arrival
was a clear signal that Wigan now meant business.

Though his first two Wembley appearances were at full-
back, it was always clear he would be a half-back. He moved
to stand-off when the club signed Andy Gregory and the two
quickly became one of the most lethal half-back combinations
in the world, blessed with a telepathic understanding and the
full complement of talent, they formed – with Hanley – a
midfield triangle that Wigan (or anybody else for that matter)
will struggle to match again. When Gregory left, Shaun
moved to scrum-half, proving just as effective alongside the
New Zealanders Frano Botica and Henry Paul and, as a senior
figure in a superstar team, he grew in stature and personality,
developing crowd-baiting try celebrations, an interest in the
cooler side of nightlife courtesy of team-mate Martin Offiah
and eventually, a celebrity girlfriend: Heather Small, singer
with the hugely successful band M People. When Dean Bell
left, Shaun took over as captain for the second time in his
career, having possibly been handed it too young at 21. The
professionalism and willpower he now brought to leadership
duties was never better illustrated than when he led Wigan to
their against-all-odds World Club Challenge win in Brisbane
in 1994.

During nearly 14 years at Central Park, Edwards became
Rugby League's most decorated player, proving himself both
the ultimate creative genius and a try-scoring machine. A
man whose courage, competiveness and fierce local pride
were unrivalled, he scored 10 tries in a match, played almost

all of a Challenge Cup final with a broken cheekbone and double fracture of the eye socket (which could have blinded him at any point), and incredibly appeared in all 43 matches of Wigan's mythical Challenge Cup run, contributing 21 tries and his first ever drop goal. However, like Boston, Ashton, Hanley et al have proved, a long Wigan career does not necessarily equal constant sweetness and light: Shaun was seen as a complex character, was accused of being difficult to coach and endured a spell where, incredibly, he was made to feel so unloved by a section of the Wigan crowd he handed in a transfer request. These days, despite becoming part of the furniture in Rugby Union's coaching fraternity, he would be ecstatically welcomed back at Wigan – or indeed any other Super League club – whenever he so chooses.

Appearances: 467 • Tries: 274 • Goals: 27 • Points: 1,146 • Honours: World Club Challenge 1987, 1991, 1994; League Championship 1987, 1990, 1991, 1992, 1993, 1994, 1995; Challenge Cup 1985, 1988, 1989, 1990, 1991, 1992, 1993, 1994, 1995; Premiership 1987, 1992, 1994, 1995, 1996; Regal Trophy/John Player 1986, 1987, 1989, 1990, 1993, 1995, 1996; Lancashire Cup 1985, 1986, 1987, 1988, 1992; Charity Shield 1985, 1987, 1991

CROWD TROUBLE

During the 1896/97 season, Wigan were forced to close their ground for 3 weeks after a referee had been assaulted and concern was expressed about a 'wilder element' infiltrating the large crowds the club was now attracting.

After Wigan's 3–4 defeat by Hunslet at Central Park on 17 February 1904, the referee's handling of the game was so unpopular that the crowd became 'threatening', and he was unable to safely leave the ground. Police were forced to take action and the Chief Constable himself had to convey the official into a Hansom cab at the top of Standishgate and away.

Wigan took on Oldham in the 1909 Championship Final and, owing to the terrible conditions, a trick cyclist was refused permission to entertain the crowds before the match. He decided to go ahead anyway, climbed over the fence with his bike and police pursued him around the playing area unable to lay a hand on him. Eventually one officer seized a corner flag and propelled it into his front wheel spokes enabling him to be led away in cuffs.

At Knowsley Road on Boxing Day 1944, unruly spectators caused an abandonment after an hour's play. At half time, a small section of the home fans demonstrated against the referee, Mr Stockley of Leigh, and 20 minutes later, when he awarded a freak try after Wigan wing Jack Fleming carried on running to the line when both sets of players were standing still, they charged on to the field and had to be held back by the Saints team while the Wigan players rushed Mr Stockley off the pitch. The crowd lingered for half an hour, finally dispersing at the sight of a police car noisily taking away the mayor of St Helens, assuming it was conveying Mr Stockley to safety. The match was never finished with Wigan winning 12–3.

MOST DERBY TRIES

Wigan

Jim Leytham (28)

Shaun Edwards, Kris Radlinski and Jason Robinson (16)

Johnny Ring (15)

St Helens

Les Jones (21)

Tommy Martyn (16)

Tom van Vollenhoven and Ade Gardner (14)

Paul Wellens and Keiron Cunnnigham (13)

N.B. Gary Connolly scored a total of 16 for both Wigan and Saints and Kevin Iro and Alf Ellaby totalled 14 each for both clubs, so deserve a mention.

DID YOU KNOW?

In 1908, Edward Croston, a coal dealer from Whelley, was sentenced to 2 months in prison and banned from every Northern Union ground for attempting to bribe Wigan's Kiwi stars Lance Todd and 'Massa' Johnston to throw a match against Hunslet on 12 September. Meeting in a town centre bar, Croston promised the players £20 each up front and suggested they might clear as much as £100, even counting out gold sovereigns in front of them when they refused.

During the 1961/62 season, Wigan postponed their home game with Hull KR owing to an outbreak of polio on

Humberside. The town's chief medical officer was of the opinion that Robins fans coming to Central Park represented an 'unnecessary risk'.

Wigan had to play Leigh three times to get through to the semi-finals of the Lancashire Cup in 1908/09. They drew the initial match at Leigh 3–3 and looked to have gone through with an 11–5 victory in the replay at Central Park only for Leigh to object on the grounds that 'Massa' Johnston had left the field to change his jersey without the referee's permission. Their complaint was upheld and Wigan had to do it all again, beating Leigh 17–3 at Central Park. They went on to win the cup.

Tommy McCarthy was the Wigan trainer in the 1920s and also something of a character. A former weightlifter and wrestler, he was awarded the Distinguished Conduct Medal at Gallipoli in the First World War and was also at various times a clog dancer, circus gymnast, puppeteer, professional ghost, minstrel and the first man in Wigan to operate a cinema reel. Michael Maguire apparently boasted a similar CV under Craig Bellamy at Melbourne Storm.

On 7 October 1973, Leigh beat Wigan 15–2 in a dispiriting affair at Hilton Park. The turning point of the match came late in the first half when mercurial wing Green Vigo burst two tackles in a left wing sprint only to touch the ball down on the opposition 10yd line in the mistaken belief that it was the try line!

In January 1972, a Welsh Rugby Union trialist played two games for Wigan and the club kept a promise not to reveal his identity in order to protect his future. Worried about

Rugby Union 'spotters' coming to try to identify him, his performances were rationed and a picture of him in the *Wigan Observer* saw his face doctored by an artist to avoid detection. He scored a try on his debut but wasn't signed and is still now only referred to in club records by the enigmatic name 'Wyngarth'. Who was this mystery man?

As a schoolboy, Simon Haughton featured in the *Guinness Book of Records* for scoring 130 tries in a single season for Bingley Under-14s including 9 in a match at prop.

TOP TEN BAD DAYS AT THE OFFICE

11 April 1980, Castleford 21 Wigan 13 (League)
'Disaster' and 'A Night of Sorrow' chorused the local papers as relegation was confirmed. 'A personal affront to all Wiganers and a blow to the pride of the town,' wrote Joe Egan. If we'd known what was coming in the next 15 years, we'd have done the conga round Wheldon Road as the points ticked over.

14 September 1980, Fulham 25 Wigan 5 (League)
'Brand new club destroy famous old name in massive shock.' Some at the time thought this was our lowest point ever, others thought it was a fix and the more rational that Reg Bowden's team were actually a fairly decent outfit made up of seasoned pros and a complacent Wigan having day out in 'The Big Smoke' were there for the taking.

13 April 1983, Featherstone 9 Wigan 9 (League)
A trip to Post Office Road that must rank as one of the worst away trips ever following Wigan. With no police present at

the ground, young Rovers fans stoned and bottled Wigan's coaches and attacked cars. Alex Murphy was punched by a spectator calling him a 'little bastard'. ('It was lucky I had my hands in my pockets or I'd have killed him,' Murph said later). On the pitch, Wigan's Championship challenge disappeared, Colin Whitfield missed 7 kicks at goal including one which he and all the spectators were convinced had gone over. Graeme West was laid out after scoring which should have led to a 7-point try but didn't, and David Hobbs' try appeared to have been 'grounded' on Nicky Kiss's chest. On the way home a supporters' coach was pelted with bricks, cobbles and bottles, the driver having to replace windows with plastic sheeting at the services on the M62.

5 May 1984, Wigan 6 Widnes 19
(Wembley, Challenge Cup Final)

Fourteen years since their last Wembley appearance and success-starved Wigan fans were treated to their sight of a well-drilled, highly professional side led by three top-class displays from born and bred Wiganers. Sadly the side in question was Widnes.

20-year-old Lance Todd Trophy winner Joe Lydon scored two scorching long-range tries, outrunning the Wigan backs so comprehensively he looked like he had travelled back from the future to help mankind defeat the Cherry and White hordes. Keiron O'Loughlin grabbed the other Widnes try, tantalisingly juggling it as he plunged over the line and 22-year-old Andy Gregory pulled the strings like a veteran in midfield. Wigan had splashed the cash to fly Harley Davidson-riding, Viking-styled man-mountain Kerry Hemsley over from Australia – one of five overseas players in their team as opposed to Widnes's one – and the man who claimed to be 'bigger than

Texas, meaner than JR' crashed over late on for the club's first Wembley try since 1965, but the consolation couldn't hide the truth that Wigan had frozen when confronted with a big occasion and a faster, classier side.

4 February 1987, Oldham 10 Wigan 8
(Challenge Cup 1st Round)

In awful conditions at Watersheddings, Joe Lydon had the ball illegally ripped out and Paddy Kirwan scrambled over for a late, late winning try and the season Wigan should have won every single trophy didn't happen. Oldham went out in the next round and were relegated.

11 February 1996, Salford 26 Wigan 16
(Challenge Cup 5th Round)

The 8-year Wembley run had to end eventually, but who would have guessed that 100-1 ranked First Division Salford would be the team to do it? Coach Andy Gregory fired up a team including several other motivated ex-Wiganers: Scott Naylor (2 tries), Steve Blakeley (man of the match) and most poignantly, Steve Hampson, harshly discarded by Wigan on the verge of a testimonial, he produced a fine display and was left roaring exultantly from the pitch at the shell-shocked Wigan board on the final whistle. Wigan missed Mick Cassidy's tenacious tackling and had two tries somewhat harshly disallowed, but hard though it was to comprehend, they just weren't good enough on the day.

2 May 1998, Sheffield Eagles 17 Wigan 8
(Challenge Cup Final)

I was abroad for this game and have therefore never seen it. This means that like many Wigan fans, I am not entirely convinced it actually happened. I fully expect that sometime in the future historians will prove it was some sort of elaborate hoax, like Piltdown Man and the Hitler Diaries, or more likely, a mass delusion such as Orson Welles's *War of the Worlds* broadcast in 1938. For the record, Wigan were poor, complacent and Sheffield – fired by a great performance from Lance Todd-winning scrum-half Mark Aston – were a team on a mission. John Kear had concentrated on every aspect of his opponents and his gameplan was carried out to the letter and backed up by some remarkable defending. But still, we had John Monie as coach, Radlinski, Connolly, Robinson, Paul, Farrell . . . I don't understand.

18 June 2005, Leeds 70 Wigan 0 (League)

This is the lowest point, rock-bottom, it seemed like things couldn't possibly get any worse. . .

26 June 2005, St Helens 75 Wigan 0 (Challenge Cup Quarter-final)

. . . oh no, hang on a minute, they can.

29 July 2007, Catalans Dragons 37 Wigan 24 (Challenge Cup Semi-final)

We'd already booked our Wembley tickets. It was written in the stars. First match back at the stadium: Wigan v Saints. Then we ran into Stacey Jones playing like a superhero. 22–0 after 20 minutes. There was a stirring comeback but it would have been an undeserved victory. Maybe this, the Fulham defeat and the Celtic Crusaders loss in 2009 are all just Wigan generously seeing the bigger expansion picture and taking a hit to put something back for all our success.

SIGNINGS

On Saturday 20 October 1973, 22-year-old forward Alan Doran got married in the morning, signed for Wigan from local amateurs St Cuthbert's shortly afterwards and then turned out for the 'A' team against Salford that afternoon!

Castleford loose forward John Clark was signed by Wigan in January 1965 after conducting talks with directors by pit head telephone, having been 3 miles underground at the colliery where he worked.

Bill Francis was signed by Wigan as a 16-year-old for £1,500. He had come to the directors' attention playing for Featherstone U-17s in the Sunday afternoon schools games that were shown on ITV in 1963 (and to think all we get now is a *Columbo* repeat and the 'highlights' from *This Morning*).

In late 2004, Wigan splashed out on Canberra Raiders prop Luke Davico to bulk up their pack. The powerful Aussie quickly settled in, telling the media how much he loved the town and was looking forward to pulling on the Cherry and White. His Wigan career lasted 96 seconds of a pre-season friendly defeat by Salford before he seriously damaged his pectoral muscle and was advised to completely rest for 12 months, forcing Wigan to tear up his contract.

Wigan have twice been let down by the world's perceived top player. In 1986, they announced the short-term signing of Aussie superstar Wally Lewis in a deal that got the game talking and convinced Wigan's shirt sponsor, one Dave Whelan, to add an extra £5,000 to his shirt sponsorship deal in anticipation. In

1998, in an attempt to take Wigan back to the top table of RL superstardom, the club, this time backed by Whelan's wealth, offered Wendell Sailor £500,000 over 2 years to sign full-time for the club from 1999. Chairman Mike Nolan modestly described it as, 'The biggest signing in Rugby League history.' Neither man ever pulled on a Wigan jersey, however.

Wigan caused huge controversy in 1994 when they signed the youngest player ever to join a professional club: 12-year-old Darryl Lacey from St Helens club Blackbrook. The loose forward was said to have it all at an early age: pace, work rate and natural ball skills and despite the fact his mother's shop was located in Knowsley Road, young Darryl was keen to join Wigan. Sadly, injury stopped him fulfilling his potential; he never made a first-team appearance for Wigan but played for Oldham for a while before returning to the amateur game.

In April 2006, with Wigan struggling with injuries and battling relegation, Ian Millward trawled the lower leagues for low-cost signings to help out. One he picked up was Workington's New Zealand full-back Luisi Sione. He was a very popular figure at Town but had one major drawback, he was a Seventh Day Adventist, a Christian denomination who believe in the sanctity of Saturday as the Sabbath, meaning he wasn't allowed to play from sundown on Friday to sunset on Saturdays, thereby ruling him out of all Wigan's home fixtures and nearly all away. His 8-week loan trial period comprised 8 possible first-team games and he would be able to play in just 2.

In 1996, Wigan gave Widnes £80,000 plus teenage half-back Sean Long for their Tongan prop Lee Hansen. Even at the time this seemed an overpayment for a hard-working but unspectacular forward, but the club had tired of Long's off-field 'issues' and his serious knee injury. Hansen went on to play a total of 26 games for Wigan, while Long was snapped up by rivals St Helens and went on to win every honour in the game, becoming the first player to win the Lance Todd Trophy 3 times, and totalled 156 tries in 319 stellar appearances, 11 of them in Wigan/Saints derbies. He had some seriously bad hair days, though.

During the war, Hull KR back-rower Jack Cayzer played 110 games as a guest for Wigan and, in 1944, he achieved the unique feat of playing for both Wigan and St Helens on consecutive days. He was in the beaten Saints side on Christmas Day at Central Park and was back in the Cherry and White on Boxing Day.

Ged Byrne was the first player to have his transfer fee set by tribunal. Salford wanted £75,000 for the Wigan-born window cleaner, his home-town club offered £20,000 and the tribunal met them sort-of half way, fixing the fee at £40,000.

Prop forward John Barton joined Wigan from neighbouring Leigh, whom he was alleged to have signed for while on sentry duty outside the Tower of London as he did his National Service in the Grenadier Guards.

In October 2005, relations between Saints and Wigan were at a lower than usual ebb with the Knowsley Road club reluctant to engage with their rivals and their former coach Ian Millward. This impasse resulted in a bizarre transfer triangle to allow Saints hooker Mickey Higham to join Wigan. Bradford Bulls paid £70,000 for Higham but kept him for barely 2 hours before giving him to Wigan in exchange for their hooker, Terry Newton. Both clubs got a new number 9, Saints got £70,000 and everyone's a winner.

PLAYER OF THE DECADE: THE 1990s

Andrew Farrell OBE (1991–2004)

From the moment a 10-year-old football player rolled up at a Graeme West Summer School in the mid-1980s, it became clear that not only was Andy Farrell the next big thing, he was also mentally and physically tough enough to cope with all the pressures such a tag would bring. Few players can have had so much predicted for them at an early age and pretty much have fulfilled it all before their mid-20s. Farrell wasn't just talented, he was something so unique he looked like he might have been created in a Porton Down laboratory by rogue DNA boffins who were mates with Maurice Lindsay: 6ft 4in tall and in excess of 17st, he could run like a centre, pass wonderfully, possessed a brilliant kicking game and had the inspirational qualities that cannot be taught.

Already starring for Wigan 'A' team as a precocious 15-year-old, he was given a first-team debut at just 16 and a year later became the youngest ever Wembley winner when Wigan beat Widnes. It was a tribute to his skills that even in a *galactico*-laden team like that Wigan vintage, shrewd observers picked out the lanky back-row forward as the jewel in the crown. He became the youngest ever international forward when he lined up against New Zealand just 5 months after his 18th birthday and was only 21 when made Great Britain captain for their 1996 tour.

He was Man of Steel twice and winner of the Golden Boot as the outstanding player in the world in 2004, yet despite consecutive Harry Sunderland Awards in enjoyable Old Trafford wins over Saints in 1996 and 1997, Farrell didn't really come close to the medal hauls enjoyed by other local-born legends like Andy Gregory, Joe Lydon and Shaun Edwards as he played in much weaker teams, often maintaining his team's contention for honours virtually single-handedly. A top-class loose forward or second row, he had the skills to play stand-off and often did, yet in 2004 played a number of games at prop and was the form front-rower in the competition. An enforcer and leader who stepped back from no opponent, few will forget the iconic image of his return to the pitch against Leeds in 2004 – with his badly broken nose so heavily bandaged as to be almost mummified – in order to kick the vital penalties and ensure a 26–22 win, or his gladiatorial confrontation with Paul Sculthorpe in a Knowsley Road free-for-all on Good Friday that same year.

His move to Rugby Union was a shock to many and like the hero of a Hardy tragedy, his courage in leaving the area that shaped him bought mainly disappointment and frustration. No one in Wigan blamed him for accepting a new challenge, they were just ultimately disappointed that the chippier writers on the other code felt licensed to criticise him and by extension his former sport, when we all knew he was Jonny Wilkinson in Lawrence Dallaglio's body, only better than both of them.

**Appearances: 370 • Tries: 111 • Goals: 1,355 •
Points: 3,135 • Honours: World Club Challenge 1994;
Super League 1998; Challenge Cup 1993, 1994,
1995, 2002; League Championship 1994, 1995, 1996;
Premiership 1994, 1995, 1996, 1997;
Charity Shield 1995**

DID YOU KNOW?

Wigan's first Rugby League try was scored by second row Bill Yates, the first try at Central Park was scored by winger Jimmy Barr and the first try at the JJB Stadium came from Denis Betts. Wigan's first 4-point try was scored by strapping teenage centre Jeff Clare against Salford at the Willows on 21 August 1983.

Wigan's first drop goal was landed by Jimmy Walkden in the first match at Broughton on 7 September 1895. Their first 1-point drop goal was kicked by Jimmy Nulty in a 17–11 win over Warrington at Wilderspool on 27 October 1974.

Only three Wigan players have scored a try in every round of a Challenge Cup run, they are all wingers and are: A.J. van Heerden (1923/24), Henderson Gill (1984/85) and Frano Botica (1990/91).

They may only have played 16 games and there was a bit of a war on, but Wigan went through the 1940/41 regular league season unbeaten with 15 wins and a 5–5 draw with St Helens at home. They lost both first-round cup ties and both legs of the Championship Final though, so let's not get over-excited.

In the 1922 Lancashire Cup final, Wigan defeated Leigh 20–2 at the Willows with an entirely Welsh back division: Sullivan, Hurcombe, Shea, Howley, Ring, Owens and Jerram. For good measure, the pack boasted another 3 players (Hodder, Coldrick and Roffey) who had deserted the green, green grass of home as well. The 3 other forwards were the Wiganers Harry Banks and Bert Webster and Tommy Woods who, although he was born in England, was actually signed from Pontypool and had played Welsh representative rugby!

In May 1986, Wigan were struggling in the Colts Cup final replay against St Helens at Central Park, so they brought on a 19-year-old half-back who turned the game decisively within minutes, the home side eventually winning 18–9. If he seemed slightly nonchalant about victory on the final whistle, this was probably because he was already a full international, had made 2 Wembley appearances and secured a John Player Trophy and two Lancashire Cup winner's medals. He was of course Shaun Edwards and I'm told he gave his winner's medal away to another member of the squad.

JOBS

In the days before you could just write 'Professional Rugby Player', players often had varied day jobs:

Ray Ashby	shopkeeper
Tommy Bradshaw	basket-maker
Ged Byrne	window cleaner
Geoff Fletcher	pig farmer
Ian Lucas	antiques dealer
Jack Morley	dental surgeon
Brian Nordgren	solicitor
Mark Preston	insurance underwriter
Peter Smethurst	butcher
Colin Whitfield	golf club maker

WIGAN COACHES

Jim Sullivan (1932–52, 1961)
P: 815   W: 590   D: 25   L: 200

Who says great players don't make great coaches? The Welsh legend was the club's first proper coaching appointment. His superb rugby brain and insistence on the highest standards of fitness saw Wigan win both the Championship and the Lancashire Cup before the war. When hostilities ceased, 'Peerless Jim' coached Wigan to domestic dominance as well as launching a number of legendary playing careers. There were 4 Championship Final wins, 2 victories from 3 Wembley appearances, 4 Lancashire League titles and 6 consecutive Lancashire Cup final successes. A row over terms in 1952 saw him do the unthinkable in many Wigan fans' eyes and leave for St Helens, whom he took to 2 Wembley finals. After a short spell at Rochdale, he returned to Central Park in 1961 but sadly illness put an end to his coaching career after just one game back.

Maurice Hughes (1952–3)
P: 45   W: 25   D: 2   L: 18

Following Sullivan was never going to be easy and the part-time masseur from Barrow found plenty of expectation came with his full-time job and £624 a year salary. Hughes had only one season in charge, leaving Wigan with an empty trophy cabinet for the first time since the war, but having been relieved of his position he nobly stayed on as assistant to his successor Ted Ward.

Ted Ward (1953–6)
P: 124   W: 81   D: 4   L: 39

Unlike his predecessor, Ward had the advantage of having been a fine goal-kicking centre for Wigan and part of the club since 1938. This bought the Welshman some time, but not enough to manage more than a solitary Lancashire Cup final defeat (to Saints) during his tenure. Ted may not have won any silverware but like some obscure ancient king, his reign will chiefly be remembered for significant events that had little to do with him: the signings of Eric Ashton and Billy Boston.

Joe Egan (1956–61)
P: 225   W: 161   D: 3   L: 61

The first Wiganer to be club coach, Egan was a popular choice as he was one of the driving forces in Sullivan's post-war dream team. Having already coached Great Britain in the inaugural World Cup in 1954, Joe arrived at Wigan after a short spell at Leigh and soon began to return the club to some semblance of glory. He matched Sullivan's record of 2 wins from 3 Wembley appearances and took the Championship in 1960. After the Wembley defeat to St Helens in 1961, Egan stepped down to make way for Jim Sullivan's ultra-short return and went on to coach Widnes, Warrington and Blackpool.

Johnny Lawrenson (1961)
P: 10   W: 8   D: 0   L: 2

The Wigan-born physiotherapist and former Central Park wing star took the reins in a caretaker capacity when illness wrecked the great Jim Sullivan's return in 1961. Assisted by club captain Eric Ashton, he presided over a thoroughly respectable 8 victories in 10 games before the appointment of Griff Jenkins.

Griff Jenkins (1961–3)
P: 87   W: 60   D: 3   L: 24

The 47-year-old joined Wigan from Halifax on a salary of £1,000 a year having impressed the board with his record at Oldham. He began in style with a win over the 1961 Kiwi tourists, the first of a remarkable 16-match unbeaten run but, despite a Wembley appearance in 1963, he was unable to deliver the trophy that a Wigan coach always must, and, after club captain Eric Ashton came through a 6-match coaching trial period with 5 victories, Jenkins' resignation was accepted and another great era began.

Eric Ashton (1963–73)
P: 442   W: 294   D: 13   L: 135

Ashton was just 28 when Wigan made him their player-coach, forcing him to give up his job at Pilkington's in St Helens and more painfully, end his international career after 27 appearances for Great Britain and England. Already one of the finest players in the club's history, his coaching career cemented him as one of the handful of almost stained-glass window worthy Central Park saints. Eric delivered 3 Wembley finals (1 victory), a League Leader's Trophy, a Lancashire League, 2 Lancashire Cups and a BBC2 Floodlit Trophy triumph. Wigan also broke the record for the most consecutive league wins with 31 (the last 8 matches of 1969/70 and the first 23 of 1970/71). Eric stopped playing in 1969 but continued as coach until 1973 when he ended an 18-year association with Wigan. He later coached Leeds, Saints, Lancashire, England and Great Britain before becoming a director at Knowsley Road.

Graham Starkey (1973–4)
P: 40   W: 18   D: 3   L: 19

Starkey came from Oldham with the unenviable task of following Eric Ashton but made a fine start with a Lancashire Cup final victory over Salford in just his tenth game in charge. However, a league campaign that ended with Wigan only 2 points above the relegation zone inevitably did for him and he left to join Rochdale Hornets before eventually returning to the comforting bosom of Watersheddings.

Ted Toohey (1974–5)
P: 19   W: 11   D: 0   L: 8

The 49-year-old former Wigan scrum-half took over temporarily in the wake of Starkey's departure. As a player once coached by the almost mythical Jim Sullivan, it was hoped Ted might have picked up some precious coaching know-how, but Wigan didn't bother waiting to find out, dumping him in January 1975 not long after a festive defeat by St Helens.

Joe Coan (1975–6)
P: 59   W: 36   D: 3   L: 20

A former schoolteacher and Saints player, Coan was the opposition coach during the painful 1966 Wembley defeat. The improvement he made to Wigan's shape and a second-place league finish in 1975 meant he was close to being forgiven that, but when trophies didn't arrive the following year, he made way for another St Helens import.

Vince Karalius (1976–9)
P: 126   W: 64   D: 5   L: 57

Desperate to reverse their decline, Wigan were not too proud to look to Knowsley Road once again, even if it meant courting Saints bogeyman Vince 'The Wild Bull of the Pampas' Karalius, an internationally celebrated hard man whose craggy features personified Rugby League's mean-street toughness in that era. Like some sort of bad movie opening, Karalius first had to be talked into taking time away from his successful scrap metal business to do 'one more job'. Wigan's potential eventually won him round and his intimidating presence and ahead-of-his-time fitness levels were expected to be just the ticket to bring a return to the halcyon days, but the big man was continually frustrated by a playing staff and a set-up below his expectations and he walked away just before a failing side reached its nadir.

Kel Coslett (1979–80)
P: 27　W: 8　D: 3　L: 16

One Saints legend departed, yet another strode in, this time it was Welsh points machine Kel Coslett. He turned down other tempting offers to pick up the poisoned Central Park chalice, even foregoing a formal contract. Despite such willing, Kel was no more the saviour than his predecessors and it seems somehow fitting that a man so closely associated with our bitterest rivals should be at the helm for our very worst moment. The failing players were not his signings and he tried hard, but first-round exits in the Floodlit Trophy and the Challenge Cup were followed by the numbing reality of relegation and Coslett's fate and place in history were sealed.

George Fairbairn (1980–1)
P: 34　W: 23　D: 3　L: 8

Wigan's fourth player-coach had a refreshingly simple brief: 'Get us up, George'. At 25, the youngest man to take the job, Fairbairn kept his part of the bargain as Wigan finished runners-up behind York and duly bounced back, also somehow managing to make a Lancashire Cup final appearance along the way. Fairbairn was promptly replaced as coach and left unhappily for Hull KR and the sort of success he always deserved.

Maurice Bamford (1981–2)
P: 35   W: 14   D: 0   L: 21

The impressively moustached Yorkshireman endured a fairly inevitable season of struggle back in the big time, with a still-weak team toiling against the backdrop of a new board of directors settling in at Central Park. Bamford made questionable use of an £80,000 transfer budget and Wigan came perilously close to returning to the division from whence they came, but the crowds tentatively began to rise, hinting that perhaps something large was slowly gathering a bit of momentum and for this reason he remains a popular figure in the club's history. His spell did his profile no harm as he went on to be coach to Leeds and Great Britain.

Alex Murphy (1982–4)
P: 82   W: 49   D: 4   L: 29

As we've seen, the combination of St Helens hero and Central Park coaching job is not a good one and it is difficult to imagine a more divisive appointment than Wigan's 1966 Wembley tormentor. Wigan's first choice was apparently Doug Laughton but the outspoken Murphy vowed to start turning up some silverware and bringing back the crowds and it was clear things certainly weren't going to be dull. His first season brought success in the John Player final – greeted like VE Day by trophy-starved Wigan fans – and his second took the club to Wembley for the first time since 1970. There were some exotic(ish) signings from overseas, some shrewd purchases from nearer home and enough tales, soundbites and apocrypha to pad out a hundred after-dinner speeches. Murphy's whirlwind tenure came to an end after the 1984 Wigan Sevens with a departure as inevitable as it was – allegedly – dramatic.

Colin Clarke and Alan McInnes (1984–6)
P: 89　W: 65　D: 4　L: 20

Unable to replace Murphy with a similar-sized personality, Wigan simply combined two. Already working at the club, Clarke and McInnes were an unusual but ultimately successful duo – the latter a quiet schoolmaster and tactician, the former an ultra-competitive motivator with an impeccable 15-year history at the club. Working on a part-time basis, they blended a host of stars from all over the world into a squad that won a Lancashire Cup, a John Player Trophy and the longed-for Wembley victory in a style few Wigan fans dreamed they'd see again. However, the board's next masterplan involved a full-time coach with new ideas, probably from overseas.

Graham Lowe (1986–9)
P: 130　W: 104　D: 3　L: 23

A charismatic and emotional 39-year-old Kiwi who turned Wigan from slowly rousing giant into rampaging superstars, the club's first overseas appointment managed to win every trophy at some point in his 3 seasons, built up the club's depleted youth structure and enhanced an already impressive reputation. His record as New Zealand national coach meant that great players – Ella, Dowling, Lewis – were keen to play under him and sought-after New Zealanders – Dean Bell, Kevin Iro, Adrian Shelford – were willing to alter previous ambitions to join his Central Park revolution. Lowe successfully switched Ellery Hanley to the pack and moulded a team of complicated egos into trophy machines, winning 4 consecutive Lancashire Cups, 3 John Player Trophies, 2 Challenge Cups, the Premiership and the League. Their 29-match winning run in all competitions between February and October 1987 was a Rugby League record, the 28th of those saw them crowned World Champions after defeating Manly on a fabled Central Park night and inevitably, the losing Australian club took note of the victorious coach and coaxed him into a return Down Under at the end of the following season.

John Monie (1989–93, 1998–9)
P: 218   W: 173   D: 4   L: 41

Matching Graham Lowe's extraordinary reign would surely be impossible, but after scouring the world, Wigan found a man who could not only do that but actually make it look like underachievement. John Monie was a dapper, pocket-sized Australian with a fine record at Parramatta where he initially learned his trade from the incomparable Jack Gibson. He twice turned Wigan down but Maurice Lindsay's persistence paid off and the two men kick-started an era of *Boy's Own* storylines at Central Park; players scored 10 tries in a match, kicked goals from anywhere and ran up incredible scorelines against quality opponents. A trip to Central Park became a genuine treat for the home fans. Monie left in 1993 after securing 4 successive League and Cup doubles, 2 Regal Trophies, a Premiership, a Lancashire Cup and a World Championship for good measure. Certainly he inherited a champion side and walked into a professional set-up, but his rigorous application of Australian fitness regimes, technical analysis and big-match know-how ensured Wigan were always ahead of their improving opponents. His methods and results built on Lowe's work to help change British Rugby League forever and played a large part in closing the gap between the British and Australian games.

They always say never go back, but the Australian Napoleon of coaching was persuaded to return in 1998 and promptly ensured Wigan topped the league and won the inaugural Super League Grand Final. However, the players and the set-up were not quite at the levels he had previously enjoyed and when results started to falter, he refused a 'director of rugby' role at the club and walked away.

John Dorahy (1993–4)
P: 41   W: 32   D: 0   L: 9

'Joe Cool' was about to take up a managerial position with a poultry firm in Canberra when he was unexpectedly offered the Wigan job. The board chose him ahead of two other Australians – Featherstone coach Steve Martin and Leigh's Steve Simms – after he gave a very impressive interview. He had played for Hull KR and was player-coach at Halifax in 1989/90 taking the Division Two club to a bad-tempered Regal Trophy final meeting with Wigan, leaving several of his new charges hoping he had a short memory or a forgiving nature. Since the players were no doubt expecting a Tim Sheens or Warren Ryan type big name from the NRL, it didn't take long for Dorahy to start feeling the pressure. He probably tried to change too much that clearly didn't need changing and took stands against superstar players such as Offiah, Edwards and Bell leading to dressing room unrest. Dorahy still delivered another League and Cup double but an ill-advised sound bite: 'To all the doubters – suck!' after the former and a scuffle with chairman Jack Robinson on the Wembley coach after the latter saw him sacked before the end of his first season.

Graeme West (1994–7)
P: 102   W: 91   D: 2   L: 9

The giant New Zealander and 'A' team coach was the natural choice when Dorahy was fired and, with a potential three rounds of the Premiership and a World Club Challenge in Brisbane in his in tray, he had the chance to make a pretty powerful case for the role full-time. 'Westy' promptly delivered both trophies and was rewarded with the job. The following season – 1994/95 – saw Wigan produce some of their greatest rugby, securing the first ever 'Grand Slam' of prizes available: Regal Trophy, League, Challenge Cup and Premiership. The team were also selected as 'Team of the Year' at the BBC Sports Personality of the Year awards and set a Rugby League record points tally for all games in a single season (1,735 from 45). It looked like West had the job for as long as he wanted it, but the unexpected end of the club's record Challenge Cup run at Salford and with it, the vital annual Wembley cash-cow led to financial problems and a failure to make a mark in the new summer season. West, like Monie second time round, was offered a director of rugby role and he declined and left.

Eric Hughes (1997)
P: 33   W: 19   D: 0   L: 14

Yet another St Helens coach who came to Wigan and wasn't successful, Hughes did his best at a club struggling financially and had his moments. There was a fine win over high-flying Bradford at Odsal and a 65–12 victory at Knowsley Road that won't be soon forgotten by either set of supporters. However, a catastrophic row with Shaun Edwards and defeats by the likes of Salford, Paris, London and Sheffield meant his departure was inevitable, although the alleged means of communicating it – a note pinned to his car windscreen – might have been better handled.

Andy Goodway (1999)
P: 16   W: 11   D: 1   L: 4

One of Wigan's finest ever second rows, Goodway was already in situ as John Monie's assistant and, as a former Great Britain coach with a Test win over Australia under his belt, possessed a fairly compelling CV. A complex character who as a player revelled in the nickname 'BA' (Bad Attitude) because of an almost punk rocker-style contrariness, his players found him difficult to fathom. Goodway won at St Helens in his opening game – never a bad start – beat table-topping Bradford and ensured the club's last match at Central Park ended in victory, but his failure to win a trophy on top of an embarrassing defeat in the brand new JJB Stadium's opening fixture saw club owners Dave Whelan and Maurice Lindsay send him on his way.

Frank Endacott (2000–1)
P: 45   W: 33   D: 2   L: 10

An avuncular and much-loved Kiwi, 'Happy Frank' put the fun back into the Wigan squad, ensuring his players were a content, bonded unit and this approach initially worked on the field. There was no Challenge Cup appearance, but the Warriors were a model of consistency in the league, finishing top of the table by 3 points from St Helens only to lose to their rivals in the Grand Final. Failure to win a trophy meant a devastated Endacott paid with his job early in 2001 after a 31–30 defeat at Salford. Perhaps Endacott's novel, amiable approach proved his downfall as the players eventually came to see him less as a demanding boss and more an easy-going friend.

Stuart Raper (2001–3)
P: 82   W: 59   D: 2   L: 21

The man whose Castleford team had ruined Wigan's first game in their new stadium took over from Endacott and his abrupt, calculating style provided an immediate contrast to his predecessor. Raper wasn't popular with all his players – Ricky Bibey famously grappled with him in what the *Guardian* amusingly described as 'Wigan nightspot The Cherry Gardens' – however he did at least bring the first piece of silverware to the JJB – a Challenge Cup final victory over St Helens no less – buying him the goodwill other recent coaches hadn't enjoyed. In 2003, he announced plans to return to Australia with his young family at the end of the season but Wigan decided to act swiftly and parted company with him early in July of that year.

Mike Gregory (2003–4)
P: 26   W: 19   D: 2   L: 5

Raper's sudden departure led to his hugely popular assistant, former Great Britain captain Mike Gregory, taking charge, initially on a caretaker basis. Only the fourth Wigan-born coach in the club's history and the first since Colin Clarke, it was a job Gregory had always dreamed of and he promptly inspired a glorious 11-match unbeaten run all the way to the Grand Final. Wigan became the first team from outside the top two to reach the end-of-season showpiece where unfortunately they just ran out of steam against Bradford Bulls.

Not a Monie-like tactician, Gregory's philosophy was concentration on defence allied to passion. His players respected him enormously and were desperate to play for him. Tragically his dream was to be cut short, in 2004, just after Wigan had narrowly lost out to St Helens in the Challenge

Cup final, the form of motor neurone disease he contracted from an insect bite in Australia led to his departure from the role and was to eventually claim his life at the age of just 43 in 2007.

Denis Betts (2004–5)
P: 38   W: 22   D: 3   L: 13

Gregory's assistant was another of Wigan's all-time greats, Denis Betts, a keen student of the game who had long been suggested as a potentially first-rate future coach. He tried to steer the club through a rocky patch with Mike Gregory still keen to come back to work against the wishes of the board. Betts was perhaps too close to some of the players, having been their team-mate not long before and when St Helens suddenly sacked their hugely successful coach, Ian Millward, Wigan decided to pounce, relegating Betts to assistant.

Ian Millward (2005–6)
P: 24   W: 9   D: 0   L: 15

There have been many St Helens players and coaches who have come to Wigan, some remembered more fondly than others, yet none can have done as much damage in as short a space of time as Millward. As an unapologetic, controversial and (worst of all) successful St Helens coach, 'Basil' was a natural hate figure for Wigan fans, but since he was also clearly an original thinker and skilled motivator, they were curious to see what he could do. Sadly, what he did do turned out to be creating dressing room disharmony, obliterating the club's record defeat on successive weekends and leaving the mid-ranking, play-off-bound side he inherited staring at the virtual certainty of relegation.

Brian Noble (2006–9)
P: 120   W: 68   D: 4   L: 48

In 2006, rock bottom of the Super League with only 1 win from their opening 10 league fixtures, desperate Wigan showed typical ambition in securing their Red Adair: Brian 'Nobby' Noble was the trophy-laden coach of World Champions Bradford Bulls, Great Britain coach and rumoured to be interesting several Australian clubs. On the face of it he had no reason to go anywhere, but the challenge and the contract he was offered by Wigan convinced him to become the Warriors' seventh coach in as many years. The board immediately backed him with cash as he persuaded his former charge Stuart Fielden – then rated as the world's leading prop – to follow him over the Pennines in a stunning £450,000 cash deal. Despite the added headache of a late season points deduction for the previous season's salary cap infringements, Noble kept the club in Super League and began a precarious rebuilding process. The next three seasons saw a mixture of highs and lows – some great displays, some not so great – with Wigan capable of beating anyone on their day but unable to match St Helens or Leeds when it really mattered. In 2009, new owner Ian Lenagan decided that after 3 play-off and 2 Challenge Cup semi-final defeats, the time was right for a new man at the helm.

Michael Maguire (2009–)

35-year-old Michael was Craig Bellamy's assistant at Melbourne Storm before becoming Wigan's eighth overseas coach and fifth from Australia in October 2009. Credited with playing a major role in Storm's 4 successive Grand Final appearances, he wasted no time overhauling Wigan's coaching and fitness set-ups on confirmation of his appointment, striving to improve conditioning, defence and game management across the board from first team to scholarship. He also shrewdly employed passionate Wiganers Shaun Wane and Kris Radlinski as his assistants to instil the right kind of pride and outlook back in the jersey.

NOGGY'S NIGHTMARE

In 1946, Wigan were widely acknowledged as the best team in the country having topped the League and Lancashire League tables and won the Championship play-off, so they went into their second Wembley final full of confidence despite the absence of four of their stars – Joe Egan, Ken Gee, Martin Ryan and Ted Ward – who were on board aircraft carrier HMS *Indomitable* en route to Australia with the Great Britain touring team. Times were hard post-war and the squad were split up across three different hotels and asked to bring their own food during their London stay. Ryan's replacement at full-back, Jack Cunliffe, was suffering from a stomach upset from his war service in the Far East and shouldn't have played, so coach Jim Sullivan offered to step in but the board refused the 42-year-old's offer.

Sadly, Kiwi wing Brian Nordgren – scorer of 2 fine tries – was handed the kicking duties and missed 7 attempts at goal, any one of which would have given Wigan the cup if converted as a 79th-minute Wakefield penalty won them the cup 13–12. The devastated Nordgren declared himself 'the unhappiest man in London' especially with the knowledge that the game's greatest ever kicker Jim Sullivan could have been playing but for the obduracy of chairman Harry Platt.

PLAYER OF THE DECADE: THE 'NOUGHTIES'

Kris Radlinski MBE (1993–2006)

Kristian John Radlinski might have a Polish name but he couldn't be more of a Wiganer if Ged Byrne cleaned his windows and he launched his own brand of pea wet. One of a handful of truly world-class players to have worn the Cherry and White since the turn of the millennium, Radlinski could almost have passed for a member of Wigan's glorious 1920s team beamed down to the glitzy, modern world of Super League: it wasn't just the neat haircut and collier's pallor, he also possessed a distinctly old-fashioned sense of fair play coupled with a beatific pride in his home town and the meaning of the shirt.

Speedy, safe under a high ball and as good a defender as has played for the club, 'Rads' earned the respect and gratitude of all in the game by turning down several huge-money offers from Rugby Union and had already achieved legend status when a persistent knee injury forced his retirement in 2005 at the age of just 29. However, he sealed proper hushed-tones greatness when, with Wigan staring down the barrel of relegation, he came out of retirement to hobble – without payment – through 6 vital matches, lending his experience, inspirational skills and sheer defensive solidity to ensure Wigan won 5 of those games and were safe before bowing out again. It was no coincidence that he was awarded the MBE the following year.

A former St Patrick's and St Judes amateur from Marus Bridge, he joined a Wigan Academy team stuffed with stars from around the region and dedicated himself to working as hard as possible in a bid to make the first team. A debut in an infamous 46–0 defeat at Castleford under John Dorahy was his only outing in 1993/94 but the following season saw him become a regular on the wing and when Va'aiga Tuigamala withdrew from the 1995 Premiership Final side against Leeds, he replaced him at centre and went on to become the first man to score a hat-trick in a Premiership Final and at 19, the youngest ever winner of the Harry Sunderland Trophy.

By the time Super League started he was already established as a rock-solid full-back and during the farcical World Club Championship tournament in 1997, he was one of the few British players to emerge with any real credit. When Jason Robinson moved to Union, he increased his already hugely effective support play to become Wigan's leading try-scorer in 2001 and 2002. He will be remembered for one of the most heroic Challenge Cup final performances of all time in 2002, winning the Lance Todd Trophy for 80 minutes of stupendous cover tackling and rollicking counter-attacking, despite having spent much of the build up in hospital on a drip with a badly swollen foot and only being passed fit an hour before kick-off after some gruesome slicing and draining. He also scored the first really legendary try at Wigan's new stadium and, Michael Maguire hopes, will be instilling in the next generation of Wigan players what it takes to make it at Wigan and what it means when you do.

Appearances: 322 • Tries: 183 • Goals: 1 •
Points: 734 • Honours: Super League 1998;
Rugby League Championship 1994/95, 1995/96;
Challenge Cup 2002; Premiership Trophy 1995, 1996,
1997; Regal Trophy 1995/96; Charity Shield 1995

ACTING UP

On Friday 28 July and Monday 31 July 1978, filming took place at Central Park for the opening scenes of a new Granada TV drama called *Fallen Hero* written by local writer Brian Finch. The drama's lead actor, Del Henney, had been training with Wigan for 3 weeks in order to convince as a Rugby League professional and Wigan coach, Vince Karalius, was the programme's technical adviser. Wigan fans were encouraged to don club replica shirts and turn up to Central Park to act as 'crowd extras'.

For the match scenes between 'Wigan' and the fictional Houghton Rangers, the 26 players would be played by Wigan's actual first team and 'A' team respectively. This led to huge unrest as Colin Clarke, Dave Regan and Keith Gaskell took offence at being placed in the Houghton side (effectively branding them reserves) and Terry Hollingsworth, who did play for 'Wigan', objected to being taken off at half time. All 4 went on the transfer list that same week. That's actors for you.

DERBY GRIEVANCES

The first Wigan/Saints derby took place on 16 November 1895 and ended 0–0 (one of 6 such scorelines for the club that year). Wigan wing Teddy Flowers had what seemed a perfectly good try ruled out for a forward pass, stopping Wigan moving 2 places up the league.

On Good Friday 1993, 29,839 turned up to Central Park to watch Wigan take on Saints in a virtual Championship decider.

With the scores locked at 8–8 in the dying minutes, Joe Lydon looked to have won the game with his customary smartly taken long-range drop goal. 'Ducky' O'Donnell, once of Wigan now St Helens, vociferously claimed to have touched the ball in flight as he dived and it was disallowed. Replays showed he had got nowhere near it and the controversy became known as 'The hand of G.O.D.' (Gus O'Donnell).

On 27 December 1932, Saints beat Wigan 13–10 at Knowsley Road but their winning try caused uproar for months with seemingly everyone bar the referee and the scorer, loose forward Walter Groves, convinced he had been grounded 2 yards short.

In the 1971 Championship Final at Station Road, Wigan took on St Helens and, thanks mainly to a majestic all-round display from second row Bill Ashurst, with 7 minutes left and their opponents down to 12 men, they comfortably led 12–6. However, a converted Bob Blackwood try gave Saints impetus and John Walsh ambitiously tried to win the game with a long-distance drop goal; his attempt fell short but centre Billy Benyon – struggling with an injured shoulder – had followed up and took the bouncing ball to score the winning try despite Wigan's vehement protests that Benyon was clearly offside.

On 9 July 2000, St Helens came back alarmingly from 16–0 down at the JJB but, with 4 minutes to go, thankfully it appeared Tommy Martyn had lost the ball as he jinked over the line. Wigan relief soon turned to disbelief when after an agonising delay, the video referee ruled Lee Gilmour had dislodged it and awarded the smirking stand-off his hat-trick try and Saints a 30–28 win.

In the 2004 Challenge Cup final in Cardiff, Saints' Sean Long came back to haunt his home-town club on the biggest stage carrying off the Lance Todd Trophy with 6 goals and an impressive all-round display in the 32–16 win despite sporting a bizarre Björn Borg-style white headband and matching 1970s hair throughout. However, Wigan did have 2 tries disallowed and their opponents' opening score came from Jason Hooper charging down a Radlinski kick when clearly offside, but fair's fair (clench teeth) Saints and Long were just too good on the day. This defeat levelled the score at 3–3 in Challenge Cup finals between the two old rivals.

In the late 1980s, relationships were at an all-time low between the two clubs, there was controversy when Saints fielded a seriously weakened side on Good Friday 1987, Saints angered Wigan by voting in favour of admitting Springfield Borough (a lower division club based at Wigan Athletic's Springfield Park ground) and brought an acrimonious High Court case over Adrian Shelford's transfer which Saints lost at considerable expense. Saints were accused of spying on training sessions to make sure the big Kiwi prop wasn't breaking the terms of his court order. Wigan players were attacked on the Knowsley Road pitch on Good Friday 1988 and with sniping from Murphy in the press, Graham Lowe was said to be close to quitting.

1966 AND ALL THAT

21 May 1966, Wigan 2 St Helens 21
(Challenge Cup Final at Wembley)

Making their second successive Wembley appearance Wigan
were originally confident of gaining revenge for 1961 and a
record crowd of 98,536 paid up well in advance to enjoy what
promised to be a blood-and-thunder Derby on a national stage.
Instead they were treated to a dreadful farce of a game that
will be remembered only for cynicism and as a sad Wembley
farewell for the likes of Boston, Ashton and McTigue. Prime
Minister Harold Wilson, guest of honour, must have privately
decided that never mind a week in politics, 80 minutes could
be an interminably long time in Rugby League.

In the days when scrums meant something, both sides
realised the 2-match suspension of hooker Colin Clarke
just before the final was a cataclysmic event, utility forward
Tom Woosey would be forced to fill in meaning Saints with
their hooker Bill Sayer – ironically a Wigan player earlier that
season – had a potentially huge advantage in the scrums. Alex
Murphy, the St Helens skipper, realised that any penalty should
be kicked into touch as from the resultant scrum, Saints would
be on top. Murphy continually placed himself offside, Wigan
kicked to touch and Sayer usually won the ball back for
St Helens. Wigan only twice got possession outside their own
half, as every time they threatened, their opponents simply
walked offside. The referee, Harry Hunt, spoke to Murphy
three times but he was allowed to get away with it and the
result was a dull, one-sided final still widely agreed to be the
worst since the war. South African Len Killeen secured the
Lance Todd with a try and 5 goals including one monster
penalty from more than 60yds.

As a direct result, the Rugby League changed the rules so that a tap penalty and not a scrum followed a kick to touch. Coincidentally, the Rugby League's vote on the rule change came out 21–2 in favour! Wigan fans understandably blamed a gloating Murphy and a reticent referee but on reflection considered that perhaps not buying any sort of stand-in hooker at some point during the season was something of an error by the club.

Wigan: Ashby, Boston, D. Stephens, Ashton, Lake, Hill, Parr, Gardiner, Woosey, McTigue, Gilfedder (g), A. Stephens, Major

THE LUCK OF THE DRAW

New Year's Day 1981 saw one of the most remarkable finishes at Central Park as Blackpool Borough took on Wigan. The visitors were 11–5 down at half time but rallied magnificently to lead 13–11 in injury time. They had 5 players missing through injury and had had 3 tries disallowed but still got themselves in front and heroically resisted a late Wigan onslaught. The hooter sounded and ecstatic Borough fans rushed on to the pitch to acclaim a famous victory only to find referee Mike Beaumont had awarded Wigan a penalty for a head-butt by loose forward John Corcoran just seconds before the hooter. The kick had to be taken before the game could end and full-back David Walsh promptly stepped up to level the scores and earn Wigan surely their least-deserved draw of all-time.

TEN 'AGAINST ALL ODDS' PERFORMANCES

13 May 1950, Wigan 20 Huddersfield 2
(RL Championship Final at Maine Road)

It might not have been as spectacular as Wembley 1985, it didn't take place in Australia and wasn't against St Helens, but still this display by a heavily depleted side against their full-strength nearest rivals is in many ways Wigan's finest hour. Missing 8 of their best players – Ashcroft, Bradshaw, Cunliffe, Egan, Gee, Hilton, Ratcliffe and Ryan who were all en route to Australia with Great Britain – Wigan's fitness and tenacity was too much for Huddersfield and a tribute to coach Jim Sullivan. Reserve team second row Nat Silcock typified Wigan's spirit; playing as an emergency wing, he opened the scoring after 3 minutes and marked free-scoring Huddersfield wing Lionel Cooper out of the game. A wonder try from Jack Broome added to other decent efforts from Brian Nordgen and Billy Blan (who lost 5 front teeth during the game) and great defence led by George Roughley led to a result that stunned British Rugby League and no doubt 8 men on a slow boat to the Antipodes.

7 October 1987, Wigan 8 Manly Warringah 2
(World Club Challenge at Central Park)

History in the making. Has there been a better night at Central Park? Has there been a better tryless game ever? An 'official' attendance of 36,895, fireworks, fights and an all-British line-up hardened by days of no-holds-barred, full-contact training soaking up everything the Aussie premiers had and throwing back more besides. The sort of electrifying occasion that made everyone else jealous and convinced a generation of Wigan stars that they belonged in any company.

13 April 1991, Leeds 8 Wigan 20
(League match at Headingley)

The culmination of one of the most incredible achievements in British sporting history. Victims of their own success, bad luck and weather, Wigan were forced to play 8 gruelling games in 18 days to try to win the League. Their opponents read like a Who's Who of potential banana skins: Saints, Castleford, Widnes and Bradford at home, Warrington, Featherstone, Oldham and Leeds away. After an exhausted-looking but courageous draw with Bradford in the penultimate game, a patched-up, beaten-up team went to Leeds and summoned a remarkably fresh-looking performance to win the title and complete 'Mission Impossible'. Shortly afterwards they limped and crawled their way past Saints at Wembley for the double. It will never be done again and it shouldn't have to be.

February 1992, Brisbane Broncos 6 Wigan 18
(World Sevens Final at the Sydney Football Stadium)

Wigan came, it poured, Offiah scored. The club flew round the world, beat the pride of the Winfield Cup thanks largely to Offiah's roadrunner impression, flew back and dragged their jet-lagged legs to a narrow victory in a crucial Challenge Cup tie against Warrington before the Aussies had time to say 'Gee, who cares about Sevens anyway?' Just another crazy Wigan week in the early 1990s.

1 June 1994, Brisbane Broncos 14 Wigan 20
(World Club Challenge at the ANZ Stadium)

Coaching changes, huge injury problems, jet lag at the end of a long season . . . the excuses were all ready. Jason Robinson starred, Billy McGinty and Neil Cowie excelled and the world (well the non-Northern part of Britain) finally woke up and realised quite what a well-kept secret Wigan were.

25 May 1996, Bath 44 Wigan 19
(League v Union Challenge at Twickenham)

A trilogy of games that were supposed to put an end to a century of prejudice, bitching and what ifs actually ended up feeling a bit like testimonial games and only really served to suggest to Union what a spiffing idea it would be to pinch Rugby League's best players, coaches and tactics. After predictably winning a game of League 82–6 at Maine Road and causing some Pimms to be choked on by entertainingly taking the Middlesex Sevens at Twickenham, Wigan took on Bath at 15-a-side at 'HQ'. The players were never going to work out the complexities of ruck, maul, line-out and proper scrums in a few practice games at Orrell, so they predictably lost, but in a team that saw 43-year-old coach Graeme West come out of lengthy retirement to join Andy Farrell in the second row just because they were the tallest two people at the club, the also-retired Joe Lydon playing fly-half because he used to now and again as a schoolboy and ex-All Black wing Va'aiga Tuigamala playing flanker because he was quite big and knew the rules, Wigan produced some great stuff when they got the chance. Young scrum-half Craig Murdock scored 2 tries that were so good, if he'd been wearing an England shirt he'd probably now have a minor West London prep school named after him.

5 September 1999, Wigan 28 St Helens 20
(League match at Central Park)

The last game at Central Park. Yes, it was very sunny, yes, it was a sell-out carnival atmosphere and yes, we got to see a parade of legends reminding us that not even demi-gods are impervious to the march of time. But if we were in denial about what was to happen afterwards, we were certain that the jubilant, Tesco-bag waving Saints had to go home defeated.

That they eventually were had a lot to do with the start – we weren't even into the 3rd minute when Jason Robinson stormed through the Saints defence and sent another great, Denis Betts, romping to the posts from distance. The main men in the Wigan 13 were clearly up for it, we were going to win. Gary Connolly got his customary jeered touchdown against his former club, Jason got 2 crackers and Wigan-born Paul Johnson scored the last. Sadly it was Saints' Tommy Martyn who actually grinned his way over for the last try scored at Rugby League's greatest ground.

18 April 2003, Wigan 24 St Helens 22
(League match at the JJB Stadium)

This was one of Wigan's most courageous performances and the victory Stuart Raper called his greatest ever. Facing a strong Saints side on Good Friday with nine regulars missing, Raper was forced to give debuts to a number of Academy players including three 17-year-olds and call on some older heads to play when not fully fit. The players did him proud on a day when records were expected to be threatened. Terry Newton led the way with 2 tries and Shaun Briscoe produced a wonderful, match-saving tackle on Darren Albert late on, typifying the young players' spirit.

6 June 2003, St Helens 34 Wigan 38
(League match at Knowsley Road)

20–0 down after just 24 minutes, this looked like becoming embarrassing for a nervy Wigan when the backs suddenly ran riot, scoring 36 unanswered points in almost as many minutes with 18-year-olds Luke Robinson (3) and Kevin Brown (2) sharing 5 tries between them for a famous away win.

21 September 2007, Bradford Bulls 30 Wigan 31
(play-off eliminator at Odsal)

After 47 minutes of this sudden-death match, Wigan were dead and buried at 30–6 down. I imagine more than a few away fans had actually left, preferring a head start on the M62 to the continuing sight of David Solomona and Iestyn Harris collecting tries and conversions. If they did, they missed the most incredible 20 minutes in the club's history. Sporting a moustache grown for charity that made him look a little like an Algerian taxi driver, Mark Calderwood scored twice and Harrison Hansen once as Wigan ran in 3 converted tries in 9 minutes to suddenly give Bradford the jitters. In the 71st minute with the gap at just 6 points, the shell-shocked Bulls frantically attacked the Wigan line, Shontayne Hape dropped the ball, Calderwood swooped on it and found 90m of open field in front of him. He promptly galloped away to the posts for his hat-trick, his every step roared on by those incredulous Wigan fans who had stayed and were suddenly veering from calling for Brian Noble's head to venerating his genius. Pat Richards added a goal and a drop goal in the remaining 4 minutes and one of the most astonishing comebacks in league history was complete.

DID YOU KNOW?

Wigan players who have appeared in the U-11 curtain-raiser at Wembley include: Neil Baynes, Denis Betts, Phil Clarke, Wes Davies, Bobby Goulding, Phil Jones, Joe Lydon and Terry O'Connor.

John Martin is not the real name of the former Wigan director, owner of the Riverside and Wembley homecoming's Mr Showbiz. He changed it from the less starry Melvyn Leatherbarrow. John's car number plate is W1 GAN.

A former pupil of St Patrick's School, new chairman Ian Lenagan has a BSc in Mathematics from Manchester University and an MSc in Magnetohydrodynamics from Liverpool University.

The reason Wigan's Wembley attendances never approached the gates for big football matches is that the authorities apparently assumed Northern Rugby League fans would be larger people and need more room.

Two Wigan players have won the Golden Boot as the world's best player: Ellery Hanley (1989) and Andrew Farrell (2004). Brett Kenny won the award in 1986. However, somewhat unfairly, the award was not presented between 1991 and 1998 when you imagine that at least two Wigan players would probably have won it.

1923/4 VERSUS 2010

Below is an interesting (?) comparison between the Wigan squads of 1923/24 and 2010, for no good reason other than their being the only seasons for which I have managed to unearth all the relevant info on all the players. Clearly there are marked differences in the squad's geographical origins and player sizes. We'll never again see a 33-man squad mainly made up of 13 Welshmen and 16 Wiganers and, in an era of 12st forwards, I imagine someone possessing Karl Pryce's stats back then would have been charging people to 'roll up, roll up' and view them in a marquee.

WIGAN 1923/24

Name	Pos	Birth-place	Height	Weight
Jim Sullivan	FB	Cardiff	5ft 11in	12st 4lb
Abraham Whalley	FB	Leigh	5ft 9in	11st
E. Atkinson	FB	Wigan	5ft 7in	11st 4lb
Danny Hurcombe	W/C	Abersychan	5ft 5in	10st 7lb
Tom Coles	W/C	Ebbw Vale	5ft 9in	14st
Johnny Ring	Wing	Port Talbot	5ft 9in	11st 8lb
James Rynn	Wing	Wigan	5ft 10in	12st 4lb
William Evans	Wing	Wigan	5ft 7in	12st 2lb
E.J. Houghton	Wing	Wigan	5ft 6in	10st 8lb
John Blan	Wing	Wigan	5ft 7in	11st 8lb
Tommy Parker	Centre	Cwmavon	5ft 5in	11st
Tommy Howley	Centre	Ebbw Vale	5ft 7in	11st
Jerry Shea	Centre	Newport	5ft 8in	11st 6lb
Syd Boyd	Centre	Wigan	5ft 8in	11st
Frank Walford	Centre	Wigan	5ft 7in	11st
George Owens	HB	Swansea	5ft 6in	10st 12lb
George Hesketh	HB	Wigan	5ft 5in	10st 7lb
Sid Jerram	HB	Swansea	5ft 7in	11st
Bob Hunter	HB	Wigan	5ft 6in	10st 7lb
Percy Coldrick	Prop	Caerleon	6ft 1in	14st
Jack Price	Prop	Swinton	5ft 9in	13st 5lb
Wilf Hodder	Prop	Abersychan	5ft 11in	13st4lb
Tom Woods	F	Pontypool	5ft 9in	14st 8lb
Fred Roffey	F	Ebbw Vale	5ft 11in	13st 4lb

Bert Webster	F	Wigan	5ft 9in	13st 8lb
Peter Molyneux	F	St Helens	5ft 11in	13st
John Hurst	F	Wigan	5ft 11in	12st 6lb
Harry Banks	F	Wigan	5ft 9in	12st
Billy Banks	F	Blackrod	5ft 11in	13st 10lb
William Whalley	F	Wigan	5ft 9in	13st 4lb
Tom Halliwell	F	Wigan	5ft 11in	13st
P. Roper	F	Wigan	5ft 9in	11st 8lb
John Sherrington	LF	Wigan	5ft 10in	12st 6lb

WIGAN 2010

Name	Pos	Birth-place	Height	Weight
Cameron Phelps	FB	Sydney, Aus	5ft 10in	14st 5lb
Josh Veivers	FB	St Helens	5ft 11in	13st 2lb
Amos Roberts	FB/wing	Kempsey, Aus	6ft 1in	14st 6lb
Martin Gleeson	Centre	Wigan	6ft 1in	14st 11lb
George Carmont	Centre	Auckland, NZ	5ft 11in	14st 4lb
Stefan Marsh	Centre	Wigan	5ft 7in	12st 3lb
Pat Richards	Wing/FB	Sydney, Aus	6ft 3in	15st 6lb
Karl Pryce	C/wing	Bradford	6ft 6in	18st 9lb
Darrell Goulding	C/wing	Wigan	5ft 10in	13st 2lb
Josh Charnley	Wing	Wigan	6ft 0in	14st
Shaun Ainscough	Wing	Wigan	5ft 9in	13st 5lb
Sam Tomkins	HB	Chorley	5ft 11in	12st 4lb
Thomas Leuluai	HB	Auckland, NZ	5ft 7in	14st
Paul Deacon	HB	Wigan	5ft 7in	12st 7lb
Joe Mellor	HB	Warrington	5ft 11in	11st 8lb
Stuart Fielden	Prop	Halifax	6ft 3in	16st 7lb
Iafeta Paleaaesina	Prop	Auckland, NZ	6ft 1in	19st 1lb
Eamon O'Carroll	Prop	Oldham	5ft 11in	15st 6lb
Mark Riddell	Hooker	Sydney, Aus	6ft 0in	15st 5lb

Michael McIlorum	Hooker	Leeds	5ft 9in	13st 9lb
Andy Coley	F	Warrington	6ft 3in	16st 4lb
Harrison Hansen	F	Auckland, NZ	6ft 1in	15st 9lb
Phil Bailey	F	Inverell, Aus	6ft 2in	15st 4lb
Joel Tomkins	F	Chorley	6ft 3in	15st
Paul Prescott	F	Wigan	6ft 3in	16st 4lb
Lee Mossop	F	Whitehaven	6ft 3in	16st 2lb
Liam Farrell	F	Wigan	6ft 1in	14st 7lb
Ben Davies	F	Leigh	6ft 1in	15st
Chris Tuson	F	Leyland	6ft 0in	14st 4lb
Jonny Walker	F	Preston	6ft 2in	13st 1lb
Sean O'Loughlin	LF	Wigan	6ft 2in	16st 2lb

WHAT WIGAN HAVE WON

1 Grand Final, 1 BBC2 Floodlit Trophy, 1 Emergency War League, 1 League Leader's Trophy, 3 World Club Challenges, 4 Charity Shields, 6 Premierships, 8 Regal/JPS Trophies, 8 Division One titles, 10 Championship Finals, 17 Challenge Cups, 19 Lancashire League Titles, 21 Lancashire Cups.

BIBLIOGRAPHY

Primarily the archives of the *Wigan Observer* and *Wigan Examiner* newspapers, *Open Rugby* magazine and my own anoraky records, but also the following:

French, Ray, *100 Great Rugby League Players*, MacDonald, 1989

Gate, Robert and Latham, Michael, *They Played for Wigan*, Mike R.L. Publications, 1992

Hewson, Ray, *They Could Catch Pigeons*, MH Publications

Morris, Graham, *100 Greats: Wigan Rugby League Football Club*, Tempus, 2005

Morrison, Ian, *Wigan RLFC 1895–1986*, Breedon Books, 1986

Ogden, Paul M., *Wigan Rugby League Quiz Book*, Smiths Books (Wigan), 1989

Wilson, Paul, *The Best Years of our Lives: Wigan's Rise from Second Division to Super League*, Mainstream Publishing, 1996

Winstanley, Jack, *The Illustrated History of Wigan RLFC*, Smiths Books (Wigan), 1988